EVERYTHING®
C·R·A·F·T·S
BABY
SCRAPBOOKING

*Fun and easy designs to
celebrate all your baby's firsts*

MaryJo Regier
and the Editors of *Memory Makers*

Adams Media
Avon, Massachusetts

An Everything® Series Book.
Everything® and everything.com® are registered trademarks of F+W Publications, Inc.

Published by Adams Media, an F+W Publications Company
57 Littlefield Street, Avon, MA 02322 U.S.A.
www.adamsmedia.com

ISBN: 1-59337-225-6
Printed in the United States of America.

J I H G F E D C B A

Library of Congress Cataloging-in-Publication Data
Regier, MaryJo.
Everything crafts—baby scrapbooking / MaryJo Regier and the editors of Memory Makers.
p.   cm.
(An everything series book)
ISBN 1-59337-225-6
1. Photograph albums. 2. Photographs—Conservation and restoration. 3. Scrapbooks.
4. Baby books. I. Memory Makers Books. II. Title. III. Series: Everything series.
TR465.R42 2005
745.593—dc22
2004026917

Some material in this publication has been adapted and compiled
from the following previously published works:

Baby Scrapbooks ©2000 (Memory Makers/F+W Publications, Inc.)
Quick & Easy Scrapbook Pages ©2003 (Memory Makers/F+W Publications, Inc.)
Scrapbook Lettering ©2002 (Memory Makers/F+W Publications, Inc.)
Creative Photo Cropping for Scrapbooks ©2001 (Memory Makers/F+W Publications, Inc.)

Photography by: Cambon Photography, Satellite Press: Ken Trujillo

This book is available at quantity discounts for bulk purchases.
For information, please call 1-800-872-5627.

contents

Introduction • vi

If you want to get in touch with your inner creativity but aren't sure where to begin, you've already completed Step One—choosing the perfect resource to help you get started. The EVERYTHING® CRAFTS books are ideal for beginners because they provide illustrated, step-by-step instruction for creating fun—and unique—projects.

The EVERYTHING® CRAFTS books bring the craft world back to the basics, providing easy-to-follow direction on finding appropriate tools and materials to learn new craft techniques. These clear and readable books guide you every step of the way, from beginning until end, teaching you tips and tricks to get your craft to look just right.

So sit back and enjoy. This experience is all about introducing you to the world of crafts—and, most of all, learning EVERYTHING you can!

A note to our readers:

Welcome to the exciting world of scrapbooking! You're not sure what it's all about, so you picked up this book to discover everything you need to know—and to have fun while learning the ropes. Start exploring what you need as far as the tools, materials, and techniques that will serve as a foundation for creating gorgeous scrapbook pages to cherish memories of your newborn. Use everything you find in this book to help you construct other scrapbook themes for special events like your wedding.

—The Editors, EVERYTHING® CRAFTS *Series*

Introduction

Everything® Crafts—Baby Scrapbooking is packed full of fun and unique projects that will have your friends begging for your secrets. We have featured many distinctive ideas. In addition, we tell the stories behind the pages. Included are page ideas for pregnancy, showers, name selection, birth, family, and more. We also included adoption, ceremony, and cultural pages, as well as treatments for portraits and heritage pages. And since a baby's daily activities are the equivalent of a parents' workday, we've paid extra attention to those all-important sleepy, bath, meal, and playtimes, as well as illnesses, boo-boos, and growth pages. Lastly, we have included historical and informative baby-related tips and advice.

Baby's first year bustles with rapid growth and wondrous change. Few parents can resist capturing the wide-eyed innocence, toothless grins, and miraculous "firsts" in photos. And with an estimated 4 million babies born each year, we're talking about a lot of photos.

Whether you're new to scrapbooking or a seasoned veteran, a grandparent or a parent-to-be, there is inspiration here for everyone. We hope you enjoy this same heartwarming experience as you look through and use the pages of this book.

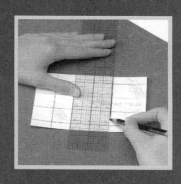

Part I

Getting Started

Tools and Materials
Journaling
Techniques

Infancy is fast-paced and filled with tender and meaningful moments. Moments that few parents, friends and relatives can resist capturing in photographs. While the thought of creating a baby scrapbook album may seem overwhelming, a little pre-planning, organization, and inspiration will make the labor of love manageable and rewarding.

1. Jot down memories that your photos inspire which may have been neglected through journaling. Sort these memories according to events or put them in chronological order, determining if you will add pre-birth photos and memorabilia into the album. You may want to enlarge some photos. Assembling sorted photos and memorabilia to be included in the album will help determine the album's size, number of total pages, and page protectors needed.

2. Albums come in three-ring binder, spiral, post bound, or strap-style. The most popular, readily available sizes are 12" × 12" and 8½" × 11". Sturdy albums will withstand the test of time. Albums should provide an acid- and lignin-free and photo-safe environment for photos and memorabilia. Expandable albums are best for making baby's album an ongoing project.

3. Your baby album's visual theme will depend on your photos and memorabilia, as well as what fits your style and budget. The repeated use of a design element, color, or unique border can give the album continuity. Shop with a list of page layouts and some photos to avoid any unnecessary spending.

4. Beautiful scrapbook pages and albums rely on balanced, eye-pleasing composition. Consider using two-page spreads that are clean and basic as opposed to making each page a unique work of art. Save elaborate designs and fancy techniques for title pages and important photographs. Some basic concepts to help your page composition follow. And remember, lay out an entire page or spread before mounting anything.

Focal Point A scrapbook page may contain several photos, but one should be important enough to be a focal point. Use the rest of the page and photos to complement the focal point.

Creative Photo Cropping Creative cropping breaks the monotony of a square or rectangular page while emphasizing the subject or removing busy backgrounds. You will find many successful examples of photo cropping throughout the pages of this book.

Matting and Framing You can focus attention on special photos with decorative mats and frames, which can be purchased or handmade with colored or printed papers, fancy scissors, and templates. Selected colors should complement photos without stealing away any attention.

Adding Embellishments Once your photos and memorabilia are in place, complete the layout by adding design embellishments such as stickers, die cuts, punched shapes and more.

5. No page is complete without your own words to tell the story. Handwritten words add a personal touch. There are also computer fonts, lettering books and journaling templates available. We have also included lettering patterns and page title ideas to help you. Try to tell your baby's story without relying solely on photos.

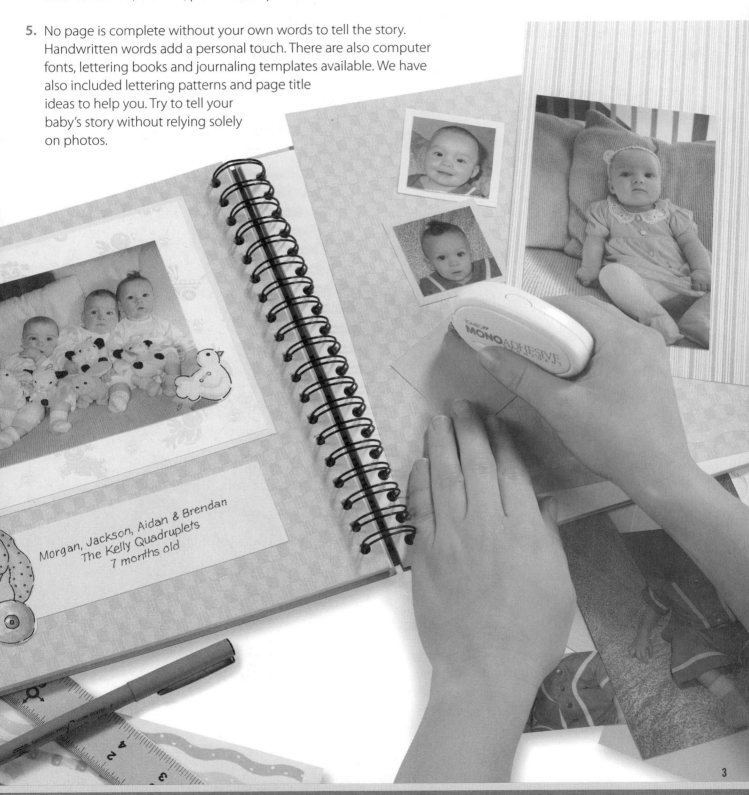

Morgan, Jackson, Aidan & Brendan
The Kelly Quadruplets
7 months old

Tools and Materials

Use these lists of basic tools and supplies and unique design additions to help you get started on your baby scrapbook album.

Albums and scrapbook pages

Colored and printed papers

Page protectors

Pens and markers

Permanent and removable adhesives

Ruler

Scissors

Unique Design Additions

Die cuts

Fancy rulers

Fancy scissors

Journaling and design templates

Memorabilia pockets

Paper frames

Paper trimmers/cutters

Photo corners

Punches

Stamps

Stickers

For preservation purposes, it is strongly recommended that you use acid- and lignin-free albums and paper products, photo-safe adhesives, PVC-free plastics and pigment inks.

Checklists

Like most parents, you will take a lot of photos and you will save everything. Use these lists as the basic framework for organizing your photos and memorabilia.

Memorabilia

❑ Baby's ultrasound photos

❑ Color-copied nursery wallpaper/fabric swatches

❑ Shower invitations and cards

❑ Squares cut from shower wrapping papers

❑ Gift list and registry

❑ Hospital bracelets, bassinet name tag

❑ Copy of doctor's notes

❑ Copy of birth certificate

❑ Foot- and handprints

❑ Birth announcement

❑ Newspaper clippings

❑ Congratulatory cards

❑ E-mail announcement and replies

❑ Letters to baby from family and friends

❑ Ceremony mementos

❑ Baby photos of Mom and Dad

❑ Heritage baby photos of relatives

❑ Time capsule souvenirs

❑ Formula, food, and diaper labels

❑ Growth and development records

❑ First lock of hair

Baby Photos

- Positive pregnancy test
- Stages of pregnancy
- Mom receiving ultrasound
- Nursery preparation
- Baby shower guests, gifts, refreshments
- Hospital and hospital nursery
- Actual birth or adoption
- Doctor's and nurses' care
- Baby with doctor or midwife
- First time Mom and Dad hold baby
- Baby meets siblings and family
- Baby's tiny fingers and toes
- Leaving hospital and homecoming
- Baptism, christening, ceremonies
- Baby in bassinet or crib
- Favorite blanket
- Nursing and mealtime
- Bathtime

- Playtime and favorite toys
- Monthly growth
- Baby with favorite stuffed animal each month
- Monthly weigh-ins and vaccinations
- Milestones and firsts
- Funny faces
- Holidays
- Illnesses and boo-boos
- Baby with family pets
- Travel and outings
- Professional portraits

Final Checklist for Tools and Supplies

Cut down the time you spend shopping for scrapbook supplies by determining exactly what you need to purchase before ever leaving the house. Photocopy this checklist and use it to preplan in order to make your shopping trip most efficient.

ORGANIZATIONAL SUPPLIES
- ❏ Photo box(es)
- ❏ Negative sleeves
- ❏ Photo envelopes
- ❏ Self-stick notes
- ❏ Memorabilia keepers
- ❏ Storage containers

ALBUM TYPES
- ❏ Strap
- ❏ Post bound
- ❏ Spiral
- ❏ 3-ring binder
- ❏ Mini
- ❏ Other
_____
_____
- ❏ Preferred brand(s)
_____
_____

ALBUM SIZES
- ❏ 4"× 6"
- ❏ 5"× 7"
- ❏ 8½"× 11"
- ❏ 12"× 12"
- ❏ 12"× 15"
- ❏ Other
_____
_____
- ❏ Preferred brand(s)
_____
_____

ALBUM FILLER PAGES
- ❏ 4"× 6"
- ❏ 5"× 7"
- ❏ 8½"× 11"
- ❏ 12"× 12"
- ❏ 12"× 15"
- ❏ Other
_____
_____
- ❏ Preferred brand(s)
_____
_____

ALBUM PAGE PROTECTORS
- ❏ 4"× 6"
- ❏ 5"× 7"
- ❏ 8½"× 11"
- ❏ 12"× 12"
- ❏ 12"× 15"
- ❏ Other
_____
_____
- ❏ Preferred brand(s)
_____
_____

ARCHIVAL QUALITY ADHESIVES
- ❏ Photo splits
- ❏ Double-sided photo tape
- ❏ Tape roller
- ❏ Liquid glue pen
- ❏ Glue stick
- ❏ Bottled glue
- ❏ Self-adhesive foam spacers
- ❏ Adhesive application machine
- ❏ Adhesive application machine cartridge
- ❏ Adhesive remover
- ❏ Other
_____
_____
- ❏ Preferred brand(s)
_____
_____

SCISSORS & CUTTERS
- ❏ Small scissors
- ❏ Regular scissors
- ❏ Decorative scissors
- ❏ Paper trimmer
- ❏ Shape cropper(s)
- ❏ Craft knife

PENCILS, PENS, MARKERS
- ❏ Pigment pen(s)
- ❏ Photo-safe pencil
- ❏ Vanishing ink pen

RULERS & TEMPLATES
- ❏ Metal straightedge ruler
- ❏ Grid ruler
- ❏ Decorative ruler(s)
- ❏ Journaling template(s)
- ❏ Shape template(s)
- ❏ Letter template(s)
- ❏ Nested template(s)

ACID- AND LIGNIN-FREE PAPER
- ❏ Red
- ❏ Orange
- ❏ Yellow
- ❏ Brown
- ❏ Green
- ❏ Blue
- ❏ Purple
- ❏ Pink
- ❏ Black
- ❏ White
- ❏ Patterns
_____
_____
- ❏ Themes
_____
_____
- ❏ Vellum color(s)
_____
_____
- ❏ Mulberry color(s)
_____
_____
- ❏ Specialty paper(s)
_____
_____
- ❏ Other
_____
_____
- ❏ Preferred brand(s)
_____
_____

STICKERS
- ❏ Themes or types
_____
_____
_____
_____
_____

DIE CUTS
- ❏ Themes or types
_____
_____
_____
_____
_____
_____

PUNCHES
- ❏ Corner rounder
- ❏ Hand punch(es)
- ❏ Border(s)
- ❏ Decorative corner(s)
- ❏ Photo mounting
- ❏ Shape(s)
_____
_____
_____
- ❏ Tweezers
- ❏ Wax paper
- ❏ Aluminum foil

RUBBER STAMPS
- ❏ Themes or types
_____
_____
_____
- ❏ Ink pad(s)
- ❏ Embossing powder(s)
- ❏ Stamp cleaner

Journaling

Try to keep a daily journal that chronicles pregnancy, birth, the adoption process and life with baby. If there's no time for journaling, jot tiny notes on a calendar to add to the scrapbook later. Other things you might wish to record:

- ❑ Reactions to news of pregnancy
- ❑ Pre-birth letter to Baby
- ❑ Name selection process
- ❑ Family tree with personal histories
- ❑ Trip to hospital
- ❑ Story of labor
- ❑ Timed contractions
- ❑ Names and comments of doctor and nurses
- ❑ Post-birth letters to Baby
- ❑ Beloved lullabies, poems, quotes and games
- ❑ Milestones and firsts
- ❑ Baby's unique habits

off to dreamland...

GOODNIGHT, MOON

Our little Angel

My 1st Haircut

Special Delivery

born to be wild

tiny fingers, tiny toes

cute as a Button

Sugar and Spice
and everything nice

Techniques

New to scrapbooking? No worries! This next section explains photo cropping and lettering techniques that are sure to make you a scrapbook expert in no time!

Negative Preservation & Storage

Creative photo cropping relies on the use of photo reprints. Organized negative storage systems make it easy to order reprints and enlargements. To prolong the life of your negatives:

- *Wash your hands before handling negatives.*

- *Wear cotton gloves to prevent scratching.*

- *Avoid cutting negative strips. Cutting ruins the emulsion, thus ruining the negative.*

- *Organize negatives like photos, either chronologically, by subject matter, or by theme.*

- *Use only 100% acid-, lignin-, and PVC-free negative sleeves, storage binders, and storage boxes.*

- *If storing negatives in an acid-free envelope, separate strips with acid-free paper to prevent sticking.*

- *Keep negatives away from dust, bright light, excessive heat, and high humidity.*

- *Store negatives in temperatures between 65–70° F with 30–50% humidity.*

- *Store negatives separately from photos; ideally in a safety deposit box.*

Photo Cropping

Any photo can be cropped, keeping in mind the precautions listed below. Cropping can be as simple as trimming a photo's corners or as elaborate as cutting and reassembling a photo into a mosaic. Working with photo reprints gives you great artistic freedom. In addition, certain characteristics of a photo can dictate the best way to use cropping to enhance the image.

Historic Photos

To truly preserve a photograph means leaving it in its original state. It's not recommended to crop one-of-a-kind family heirlooms or other old photographs. Consider the value to future generations if they are left intact. Cut duplicates of historic photos instead of the originals.

Artistic Composition

Cropping could detract from the artistic value of a photograph. Was the photographer trying to convey a certain mood by leaving extra space around the subject? Does the out-of-focus foreground lend a perspective that would be lost if you cut it out? When cropping, go slow while considering the drama of a photo's imagery.

Polaroids

Polaroid "peel apart" photos were first introduced in 1948 and are safe to cut because the final print is separated from the reactive chemicals and the negative when the photo is "peeled apart." Polaroid "integral" prints (lower), manufactured since 1972, should not be cut because the positive and negative stay together, and cutting the print would expose the chemical layers. Instead of cutting an integral print, noted for its thickness and ¾" white bottom border, use a color copy of the print for cropping.

Photo Duplication

The easiest way to duplicate your photos is by having reprints or enlargements made from your negatives. However, we often have photos for which we have no negatives. Fortunately, there are ways to duplicate photos without the use of negatives.

Take a Picture of a Picture

The biggest benefit of this method is that it creates negatives for your photos. A manual 35mm SLR camera (with an inexpensive close-up or macro lens set), or a point-and-shoot camera (with a macro lens), works great. Simply place your photo on a flat surface or tape to a wall in bright, even light, focus and snap!

Color Copy Machines

The least expensive duplicating option is to use a laser color copier, which is sensitive to the different shades in photographs. Color copiers allow you to change the size of the image. For preservation purposes, use acid-free, 28-pound or heavier, smooth, white paper. Color photocopy toner is known to be more stable than inkjet dyes, so choose color copying over printing with an inkjet printer when possible. In addition, use a mat or other barrier between layered photos and color copies of photos when possible.

Reasons to Crop a Photo

Busy photos, with lots of people and unnecessary background, take attention away from the photos' subjects. Framing and silhouetting can isolate and focus attention on your subject.

Cropping allows you to remove photo blemishes, such as glare from flashes, closed eyes, strangers in your pictures, out of focus elements, lab printing errors, and more.

Add style and variety to your page by cropping your photos into a shape. There are many shapes to experiment with, and changing the shape will also change the final effect. Give your cropped photo breathing room, however, so that the photo's content is not lost.

Herein lies the reason behind the allure of creative photo cropping—the "shear" fun and enjoyment of taking a photo and creating a new piece of art with it.

Scanning

To scan your photos at home, use the TIFF file format for high-resolution images. The quality of your duplicated photos will depend on the quality of your scanner, scanning software, printer and the paper you print on. If do-it-yourself scanning is not for you, get high-quality photo scans put on a CD at a camera store, mini lab or professional lab. To print images from a CD, a high quality color printer and photo-quality printer paper will give the best color results.

Digital Photo Machines

Digital, print-to-print photocopy machines are user-friendly, self-service machines that can be found at your local discount, photography, drug store, or supermarket. Some popular standard features include the ability to make enlargements and reductions, custom cropping, rotating and zooming in, and the ability to sharpen and adjust color and brightness of images. Some allow you to convert a color print to a black-and-white or sepia-toned photo. Many digital photo machines have the ability to write images to floppy disks and print from CDs.

Professional Photo Duplication & Restoration Services

Some specialty photography labs will make a digital copy for about the same price it costs to use a self-service digital photo machine. Some labs will charge separate prices to make the negative and print to your desired size, which could be more than double the cost of one photo machine use. Although these services can be expensive, they are worth it, particularly for reproducing valuable heirloom photos and repairing seriously damaged photographs.

Cropping Tools and Supplies

Use this list of tools and supplies to help you get started in creative photo cropping.

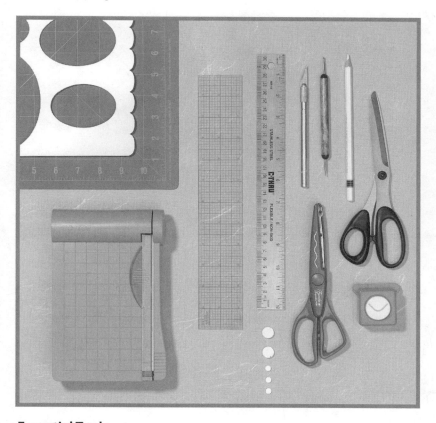

Essential Tools

Paper trimmer
Corner rounder/punches
Craft knife
Cutting mat
Rulers
Decorative scissors
Foam spacers

Shape templates
Straight scissors
Embossing stylus
Photo-safe wax pencil

Optional Tools

Clear dies used for making die cuts
Clear plastic triangles
Optical cleaning cloth and lint-free gloves
Decorative rulers
Shape cutters
Graduated templates
Aluminum foil and waxed paper
Lubricating oil

A Little Advice...

A firm hold on both photos and cropping tools will ensure precision cutting and accuracy. To improve the cutting quality of most cropping tools, simply cut through wax paper or aluminum foil several times. Remember to save your photo scraps and snippets for use in creating even more cropped photo art.

Tips & Techniques for Cropping Tools

These illustrated tips and techniques will help you achieve the best results from your cropping tools and supplies. Begin with a work surface that is clean and protected by a cutting mat. Make sure your tools are clean, dry, and sharp before you begin cropping photos.

Clear Dies Place photo face down on foam side of die, centering in see-through area. Place die foam side up on die tray; roll through machine. Push finger through hole to push photo back out of die.

Clear Plastic Triangles Various sizes of triangles can be used to make photo kaleidoscopes, with 30° and 45° angles being the most common. Clear triangles also allow for easy viewing of photos beneath.

Optical Cleaning Cloth and Gloves Remove crop lines and fingerprints from photos with an optical cleaning cloth. Wear lint-free gloves when handling negatives to prevent scratches on negatives.

Paper Trimmers Paper trimmers come in many sizes and are great for straight cuts and 90° angles. Place your index finger and thumb firmly on the photo, then bring or slide the blade down quickly and smoothly.

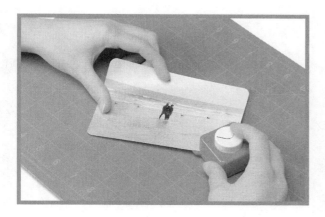

Punches, Corner Rounder Corner rounder punches are simple to use for softening the look of a photo's corners.

Craft Knife & Cutting Mat A cutting mat will protect your work surface. For straight cuts, hold the craft knife against the edge of a ruler. Use a craft knife to crop in tiny areas where scissors cannot reach.

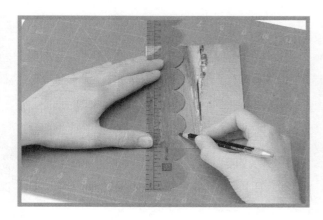

Decorative Rulers Use an embossing stylus or photo-safe wax pencil and decorative ruler on front of photos to mark cropping lines. Cut a little on the inside of the cropping line so that no markings remain.

Decorative Scissors Starting ¼" in from the base of the blade, cut using the longest stroke possible. Short, choppy strokes interrupt the scissors' pattern. Flip the scissors over to achieve a varied scissor pattern.

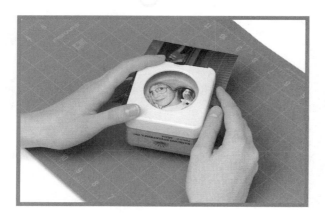

Punches Flip the punch over for easier photo movement inside the punch and accurate placement of photo before punching.

Punch Care Lubricate punches with sewing machine oil, WD-40® or punch through wax paper a few times. Clean excess oil before using punch. To sharpen punches, punch through aluminum foil.

Foam Spacers For a three-dimensional effect, place foam spacers on the back of cropped photos prior to layering and mounting on a page.

Graphing Ruler A graphing ruler can be used with a photo-safe pencil to mark grids and/or cropping lines on the back of photos when making photo mosaics.

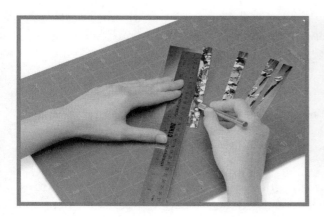

Metal Straightedge Ruler When using a craft knife to cut a line, cut against a metal straightedge ruler instead of a plastic ruler, which the knife will cut into. Hold photo and ruler firmly to prevent slipping.

Shape Cutters Practice using these tools first on paper or unwanted photos. Place shape cutters or croppers directly on photo and adjust to the desired size. Hold photo and cutter firmly to ensure precision.

Shape Templates Position template over your photo and use a photo-safe wax pencil or an embossing stylus to trace the outline onto the photograph. Cut the shape inside the cropping line so no markings are visible.

Straight Scissors Scissors should be clean and sharp. For precision, small scissors work best when silhouette cropping. Use long strokes with larger scissors to ensure a smooth cut line.

Scrapbook Lettering

Practicing the art of creative lettering requires a few essential tools that you may already have on hand.

Pencils Use a comfortable, easy-to-erase pencil for light tracing and for drawing freehand. Choose from standard pencils that can be sharpened or mechanical pencils with lead refills available in different lead weights.

Ruled notebook or graph paper Keep ruled notebook or graph paper on hand for practicing different lettering styles, whether tracing or drawing freehand.

Graphing ruler Use the lines and grid marks of a graphing ruler to help you keep lettering straight and evenly spaced.

Pens and markers Use archival quality pigment ink pens, which are fade-resistant, waterproof and colorfast.

The chart on the opposite page illustrates the variety of pen styles and the results each one creates. A black fine-tip pen is good for journaling and tracing letter outlines. A black bullet-tip pen lets you draw boulder letters and thicker outlines.

Non-abrasive eraser Non-abrasive erasers safely remove pencil marks without tearing the paper. They are available in different sizes, as well as retractable, pen-styles with refillable eraser sticks.

Paper for title and journaling blocks Unless you're writing directly on the scrapbook page, you'll need solid-colored, acid-free scrapbook paper on which to pen your lettering for page titles and journaling blocks.

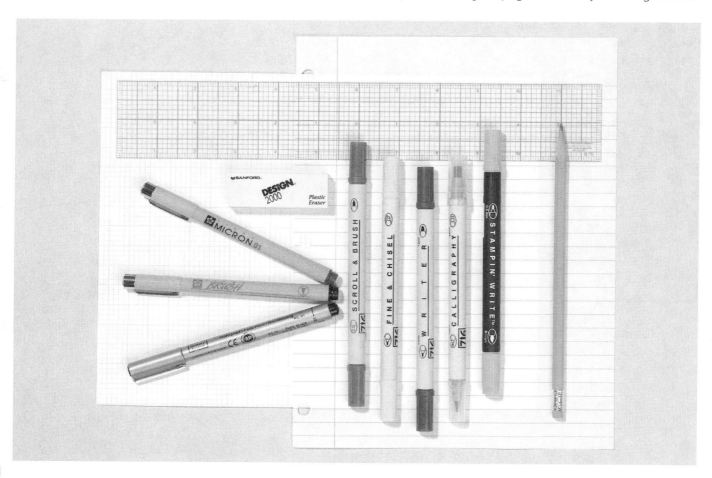

Tools for Transferring and Tracing Lettering

These optional items make it easier to trace the lettering in this book and to work with the lettering once it is traced.

- ◆ Access to a photocopier for enlarging or reducing letters
- ◆ White typing or copier paper
- ◆ A sunny window or a light box for tracing
- ◆ Removable artist's tape to anchor photocopies and paper while tracing
- ◆ Translucent paper or vellum
- ◆ Transfer paper
- ◆ Embossing stylus
- ◆ Scissors, a craft knife, and a cutting mat
- ◆ Photo-safe adhesives for mounting

Methods for Reproducing Lettering

You can re-create lettering styles through either tracing or freehand drawing. Tracing letters can help you make beautiful titles and will also help you develop the skills needed to more easily and confidently draw the characters.

How to Trace Letters

Before attempting any of the illustrated tracing methods photocopy the alphabet you wish to reproduce, enlarging or reducing it to suit your needs. If the alphabet shown in this book is the perfect size for your project, simply trace it onto white scrap paper. Once you have a complete alphabet on white paper, you're ready to trace the letters to create scrapbook titles.

Light Box or Sunny Window For light-colored papers, use artist's tape to attach your selected alphabet to a light box, sunny window or an underlit glass table. Lightly pencil guidelines on the paper on which you wish to create your title. Tape this paper atop the alphabet. Trace letters one at a time, in appropriate positions, until your message is complete.

Translucent Paper or Vellum Trace any lettering style through translucent paper such as vellum, tracing paper, or thin white paper. Lightly pencil guidelines on the paper and lay it over the copy of the selected alphabet. Trace letters one at a time, in appropriate positions, until your message is complete.

Transfer Paper Use white or yellow transfer paper to trace onto heavy, dark-colored paper. Before transferring lettering, trace it onto scrap paper, using any of the described methods. Place traced lettering atop transfer paper. Layer both sheets of paper (traced and transfer) over a sheet of dark-colored paper. Trace. Use graphite transfer paper for tracing onto light-colored paper.

Embossing Stylus If you don't have transfer paper and want to trace onto dark paper, use an embossing stylus. First trace the lettering onto scrap paper, then place the lettering over dark paper on top of a soft surface such as a cutting mat. When you trace the lettering with an embossing tool, it leaves an indentation that may be traced over with an opaque pen.

How to Draw Letters Freehand

If you are relatively new to freehand lettering, create your title on vellum paper. Place the transparent sheet over lined notebook or graph paper, then follow the underlying grids and lines to maintain consistent letter heights and spacing. Curvy, more arbitrary lettering styles are a good choice for novices because they require less precision and are more forgiving of errors.

Following, are the basic steps for drawing letters freehand. Once you recognize the different components of a lettering style, it becomes much easier to re-create. Drawing letters freehand takes practice, practice, practice!

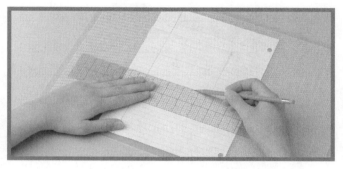

1. Use a ruler to lightly pencil any necessary guidelines, including those for spacing.

2. Sketch the basic shape of each letter without any stroke embellishments.

3. Outline in pencil any wide, thick or fill-in areas as desired.

4. Add any stroke embellishments such as curves, swirls, flowers or other details.

5. Erase and revise as necessary until you're satisfied with each letter.

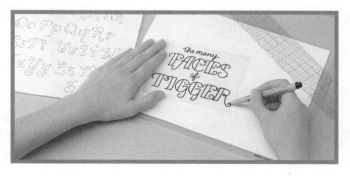

6. Outline letters with an appropriate pen, then color and embellish if desired.

Page Design Tips for Lettering

A great scrapbook page is a work of art. It showcases photos, journaling and embellishments in a way that conveys a message and pleases the eye. Use these tips to help guide you through the process of pulling together your completed page or spread. Remember that a strong scrapbook page is made even more powerful with the appropriate, beautifully lettered title.

1 Plan ahead

Determine your page layout and design before you start lettering. Consider photo selection, page theme, paper colors, embellishments and text blocks. Before permanently mounting elements, loosely arrange them on your page. Use scrap paper placeholders for the title and journaling blocks.

2 Match your page theme or style

Choose a lettering style that fits the theme and mood of the page but don't overdo it. Use elaborate letters only for very short titles, or for specific words or letters within a title. Too many elaborate letters draw attention from your photographs. If your page is formal, use a formal lettering style. If your page is whimsical, use a whimsical lettering style.

3 Determine size, design and placement

If a title is too large, it will overwhelm your layout. If it is too small, it will get lost on your scrapbook page. When designing a title, sketch it in different sizes and styles. Select a title that will work in proportion to the other page elements.

If you have a large space to fill with a short title consider matting the title several times. Or separate the letters that make up the title and mat each individually. String them across the page, inserting small embellishments such as beads, if you wish. If your title is too large for the available space, create it on vellum and mount it so it overlaps other page elements.

4 Disguise your mistakes

We all make mistakes. When it's an "oops" with a permanent pen, you can either live with it (after all, it adds character!), or disguise it. Turn a mistake into a pen stroke embellishment—such as a flower, star or other theme-related doodle—or hide it beneath a theme-related sticker or punched shape.

Part II

Scrapbook Inspiration

projects

$\mathcal{N}$ ow that you're familiar with the tools, materials, techniques, and know-how of gathering together the precious moments, souvenirs, and memories your bundle of joy has offered you, you're ready to tap into the inspiration that will help you to shape, imagine, outline, and prepare as you piece together pages for your scrapbook album.

Baby Shower

Basic punches add quick decorations to Kim's festive umbrella. Use umbrella stencil (Puzzle Mates) to create umbrella from printed paper. Trim photos to fit umbrella. Cut rectangles for gift boxes. Trim strips for ribbons and freehand cut polka dot bow. For gingham bow, punch two medium hearts and a small circle. For polka dot flowers, punch medium flowers and ¼" circles. For edge of umbrella, punch medium flowers, small circles and mini swirls. Freehand cut lavender and silver handle.

Lauren's Nursery

Sticker borders and stamped letters highlight photos of Cheri's garden-theme nursery. Start by layering photos on pale green parchment. For the title, stamp the beginning letters (Stampin' Up!) with green ink on gold paper; cut out and border with green dots. Stamp remaining letters directly on the background. Adhere fence, flower, leaf, butterfly and green line stickers (Frances Meyer). Stamp red ladybugs (Stampin' Up!).

Marie's Story

While awaiting the arrival of their first child, David and Shawnee settled on a jungle theme for baby Alexis' nursery. David asked his mom, amateur artist Marie, to design a wall mural featuring jungle animals. Years earlier, Marie had painted David's childhood room with his beloved Fantastic Four® comic book characters.

After sketching the design in pencil on the bedroom wall, Marie put everyone in the family to work. "At first they were all scared to death that they would ruin the painting," said Marie. "But with a little encouragement, the mural slowly came to life." The family painted lions, zebras, giraffes, elephants, monkeys, parrots and hippos, which Marie later recreated for a pop-up page in her scrapbook. Shawnee's favorite animals are rabbits, which you don't usually find in the tropics. "Of course there aren't any rabbits in the jungle," laughs Marie. "But our mural indeed has rabbits sitting on top of a giraffe." By the end of the day all of the novice painters commented on how well they did. Their self-affirmation didn't surprise Marie one bit. "I believe we all have artistic ability," she says. "That ability just needs cultivating."

unique baby shower games

Bingo Bingo with baby words instead of numbers.

Create-a-Caption Guests write captions for funny expressions of baby photos torn from magazines.

Decorate Onesies Guests decorate gift onesies with paints.

Dress Baby Teams dress baby dolls fast and accurately.

Fill Baby's Piggybank Guests add pocket change to piggybank when "off limit" words or actions are exposed.

Gift Bingo Bingo played during gift opening with gift words.

Guess the Baby Match each guest to his or her baby photo.

What's in the Basket Display basket filled with baby items for 20 seconds; hide. Guests try to remember basket's contents.

Name Game Forming words with letters in Baby's name.

Off Limits Certain action or word "off limits" during shower.

Rice Bowl Find safety pins in bowl of rice while blindfolded.

Round-the-Tummy Guests estimate size of Mommy's tummy with lengths of string or toilet paper.

Scrapbook Guests make baby pages for Mommy to add photos to; guests write notes to Mommy and Baby.

Shower-in-a-Box Out-of-town relatives and friends participate in gift-giving by mail; opening of gifts is videotaped or photographed and sent to "guests" with thank-you notes.

Story-Go-Round Start baby story with "Once Upon a Time. . ." Each guest adds to story; see what develops by "The End."

Time Capsule Guests bring contemporary items to encapsulate for Baby to open some day.

Whisper Chain One guest whispers baby advice to another guest. See how good the advice is once it has come "full circle."

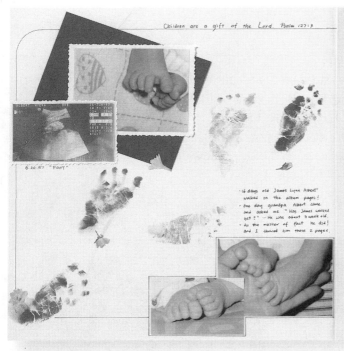

A Perfect 10!

Hyeran's son had blue feet for a few days after "walking" on her page. She suggests that an easy way to stamp baby footprints is to first tape the paper to sturdy cardboard. Then, holding the ankle firmly, tap an ink pad onto baby's foot. Carefully stamp the footprint by pressing the paper against the foot. For the layout, first crop and mat photos. Draw title with a thick black pen. Draw thin black border lines, drawing corner curves using a small round object. Adhere rose stickers (Mrs. Grossman's). Journal with black pen.

Love Letter

Karen's stained-glass technique provides a lovely frame for her one-day-old son. Start by cutting a vellum crescent for the moon. Trace a bear design onto vellum using a black pen. Color the backs of these elements with chalk. Outline the moon with black pen. To create the stained-glass window frame, cut vellum and black strips. Color one side of the vellum strips with colored chalks. Layer the vellum strips beneath black strips. Double mat photo and trim corners. Write a love letter to the newborn; adhere.

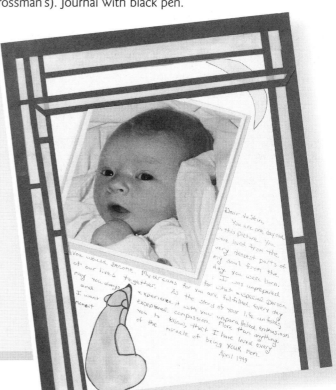

tips for better baby photos

Babies are popular photographic subjects. For the best baby photos follow these simple tips:

◆ Keep camera loaded and handy.

◆ Use the right film speed (400 inside, 200 outside).

◆ Hold camera steady.

◆ Experiment with soft, available lighting and no flash.

◆ Use flash in low light and to fill shadows.

◆ Back-lighting can silhouette Baby or highlight hair.

◆ Side-lighting illuminates Baby's profile.

◆ Get in close to eliminate busy backgrounds.

◆ Take both horizontal and vertical photos.

◆ Frame Baby off-center.

◆ Get down to Baby's level to capture perspective.

◆ Try black and white film; it's forgiving of skin blemishes.

◆ Thumb through magazines for photo inspiration.

Bride's Hanky Baby Bonnet

My son, Ethan, wore a "Bride's Hanky" bonnet home from the hospital. One day his bride can remove the stitches and use it on her wedding day.

Donna Hasker
Temple Hills, Maryland

Splashing Good News!

A duck shape is perfect for Tracy's country-style pocket page. First adhere a strip of gingham paper along the top of the background page. Draw a curved wavy line along the top of a separate page and cut away the top portion to create top of pocket. Punch ¼" holes along the wavy edge. Weave two lengths of yellow ribbon through the holes, starting from the outside edges, and tie a bow. Trace an enlarged duck die cut (Ellison) onto the pocket and cut out, creating the "peek-a-boo" opening. Adhere the pocket to the background page along the left, bottom and right sides. Using a wavy ruler, mount a wavy gingham strip along the bottom edge of the pocket. Punch small yellow ducks.

27

It's a Bouncing Baby Girl!

Julie's first granddaughter inspired these whimsical babies made with a teddy bear punch. For the background, trim white paper with large scallop scissors and layer on blue or pink. Print title and trim with scallop scissors. Round photo corners. Punch bears from flesh-colored paper, trimming off the ears. Punch an equal number of white bears, trimming into diaper shapes. Arrange babies with diapers. Draw dashed curly black lines and pink bows if desired.

News on the Day Gigi Arrived

Joyce cut and pasted articles summarizing current events on the day her daughter was born. To make her own front page, Joyce started with a headline cut from a local paper. Cut out and arrange different articles, including the birth announcement if available. Photocopy and reduce onto white paper. For the page background, trim right edge of mauve paper using a scallop ruler to draw the cutting line. Punch small hearts. Joyce then color copied and enlarged the Diaperene® logo baby; cut out and layered with newspaper.

Megan Kristine Hounsome

To make the title, Kimberley printed the letters on white paper using the Challenge Extra Bold font (Microsoft). Then she traced the letters onto the wrong side of printed paper (Frances Meyer) and cut them out with cuticle scissors. To complete the layout, cut matching strips of printed paper to border the title letters. Mat photos and the printed birth story. Write photo captions.

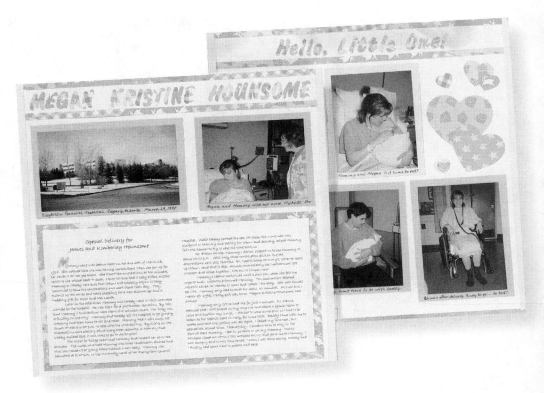

Krista's Story

A mother-to-be's worst fears came true for Krista when her water broke prematurely during her 19th week of pregnancy. During several uneasy weeks of waiting, hoping and praying, the baby maintained stability. But when Krista began having contractions, the doctors sadly informed her that their fourth child was no longer showing a heartbeat and would be stillborn. The family was devastated.

Krista found that making a scrapbook page about Elizabeth helped her in her journey of grief. "I wanted a page to honor her brief time with our family and that the kids could look at when they feel like seeing her or talking about her," says Krista. Some of Elizabeth's mementos, however, were too painful to include in the album.

Krista finds the pages are a good way to talk with others about Elizabeth. She especially appreciates the times when neighbors or family see Elizabeth's tribute. "It makes me feel better that someone is interested in her," says Krista.

Adoption

This layout honors Michele's best friend, Becky Homan, who adopted twin girls born prematurely. Start by mounting the adoption announcement across the center of the layout. Mat photos and printed journaling using soft colors and decorative scissors. Adhere baby booties die cut (Making Memories) and small punched bears. Color in printed letter outlines for the word "adoption" with colored pencils.

Babies Are Heaven Sent

Chris begins baby Joey's adoption story with a simple page showcasing his announcement card. Mount yellow triangles on page. Adhere announcement and cropped photo. Embellish with stickers (Mrs. Grossman's, Sandylion).

Adoption Album

Scrapbooks have proven to be an important tool for teaching adopted children about their past and their path, as they became part of a new family. Melanie's special album tells the story of the journey to adopt Mary, a Chinese baby girl, from start to finish: the ocean of paperwork, the months of waiting, packing for the trip to Beijing, sightseeing in China before getting Mary and meeting friends and family back in the United States.

Another fun and unique aspect of Melanie's album is her rebus journaling on the clothing page. It successfully documents the layers and layers of clothing Mary was wrapped in on the day of her adoption—a good idea since the adoption director asked for all of the clothes back except for the quilted suit seen in the center photo.

Melanie employs hand-lettered journaling, great photos and lots of memorabilia throughout the album for a truly personal touch. And Mary, now three, loves to look at her memory book. "You can never fill in all the blanks for adopted children, but it's important for her to know what a great experience it was to become a family," says Melanie. "We wouldn't have traded it for anything."

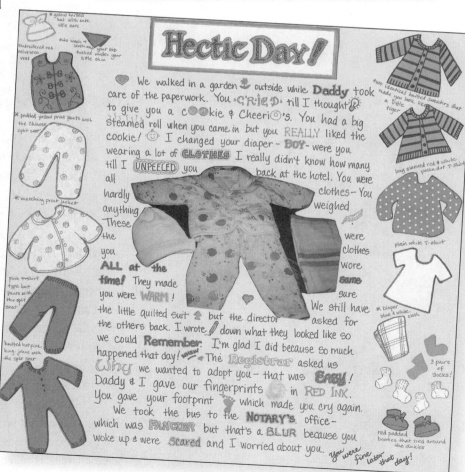

Sarah and Grandma

The dusty colors of Liza's layout create a gentle setting. Start with pale yellow for the page background. For top border, trim edges of blue strips using the Teardrop Corner Lace Edge punch (Family Treasures) with the guides removed. For title, adhere outlines of letter stickers (Creative Memories) to floral photos; cut out each letter leaving a 1/16" border. Crop and mat photos using the Teardrop Corner Lace Edge and corner rounder punches. Mat oval for journaling. Cut and layer pieces for baby in high chair. Journal with black pen. Accent title with small flower sticker (Mrs. Grossman's).

Cathryn's Story

Cathryn was returning to work following the birth of daughter Natalie and required child care for her baby and older son, Win. Luckily, Cathryn's niece Alice desired to attend the junior college near her home. Alice found a home, and Cathryn a trusted caregiver for her children.

The house was soon filled with Natalie's squeals as she played with Alice. "I could see them forging a very sweet bond," remembers Cathryn. Alice's fiancé, Aaron, and twin brother, Jake, joined her in doting on Natalie.

Cathryn's scrapbooking supplies frequently engulfed the living room table, so it wasn't long before Alice was hooked on the hobby.

Alice also provided Cathryn with welcome diversions. "We painted our toenails purple and bought toe rings, danced to Janet Jackson and watched 'Road Rules' on MTV," says Cathryn. "For me it was a yearlong slumber party."

Alice now attends San Francisco State and doesn't get to see the family as much. When she does get to visit, Natalie joyfully runs to the door calling for her cousin 'La La'.

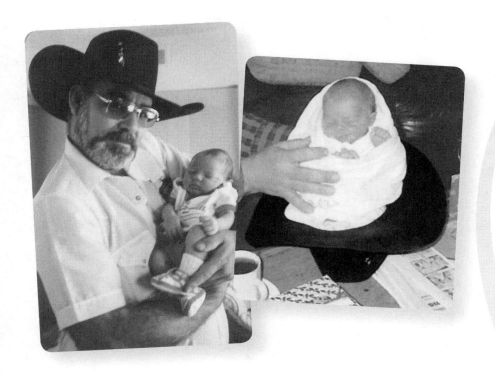

Family Tradition
My dad has pictures of all seven of his grandchildren in his coyboy hat. It's a family tradition now!

Amy Talarico
Northglenn,
Colorado

Austen and Mommy

Cindy's color photos and classic black-and-whites capture the timelessness of a mother's love. For the background, adhere border stickers (Mrs. Grossman's) on light khaki card stock. Cut a sheet of soft plum paper in half diagonally to form triangles. Crop and mat photos using decorative scissors and templates. Double mat title using deckle scissors and corner rounder punch.

Snuggle Your Daddy

Amy's page features a favorite father-son snapshot. Create the border by trimming red strips with decorative scissors; mount along top and left edges of background paper (MPR Assoc.–paper discontinued). Mount 3⁄8" strip of striped paper (Provo Craft) along top edge. Mat photo with red paper; mat again with striped paper. Cut and mat hearts using red and striped paper. Draw black line accents. Adhere gold letters (Making Memories) to red paper and cut out. Write remaining title letters with red pen.

Daddy's Little Princess

Paper piecing and punch art helped Christiane savor this father-daughter moment. Print title and mat with pink. Punch large flowers and small circles. Layer on photo mats; adhere photos. Freehand cut crowns from gold glittery paper (Sandylion), blonde hair and dresses from floral paper (source unknown). Punch large and small flesh hearts for body. Punch large and small circles for faces. Draw faces with black pen; smudge cheeks with pink chalk.

Little Sister Store

A funny "sibling rivalry" poem aptly fit the result of Kelley's attempt to photograph her two daughters. To create the "store," mat photo with blue paper. Trim bottom edge of dark pink rectangle for roof. Layer stickers (Mrs. Grossman's) along bottom edge of photo. Print the poem on cloud paper (Hallmark) and cut into a cloud shape. Cut an additional cloud shape. Mat clouds with blue paper. Adhere sun die cut (source unknown). Journal and draw blue dots.

Big Brother, Little Sister

The birth of little sister Rachel made such an impact on big brother Ryan that Jill wanted to honor their special relationship. Start with a selection of sibling photographs; silhouette all but one. Freehand cut the title letters from blue and pink gingham paper. Layer photos with letters. Journal with blue and pink pens.

My Daddy and Me Theme Album

Ruth gave each of her twin daughters a storybook of her special bond with Daddy for a one-of-a-kind Christmas gift. The books' easy-to-read captions and the fun-loving use of stamps and humor make these story-book albums a perennial favorite of Ruth's family. Note how the photos selected successfully fit the limited scope of the book—My Daddy and Me. "The girls love their stories about what they did and how they acted as babies," says Ruth.

Sewing Album

Madeline made her tribute theme album, Nannie's Dream Stitches, as a Mother's Day gift in 1998. Madeline's mother, an accomplished seam-stress, makes heirloom-style dresses for granddaughter, Ellie Claire.

My Family Tree

Heather's drawings beautifully embellish the mats and bows tying together four generations. First crop and double mat the oval baby photo. Crop remaining photos into circles using a large circle punch. Double mat each circle photo with colored circles, ovals, and rectangles. Cut bows from colored and gingham paper. Punch small hearts. Embellish mats, bows, and hearts using opaque colored pens (Pentel Milky Gel Rollers). Title page and label photos with a thin black pen.

Father and Son

Mary's son not only looks like his father but is also wearing the same blue velvet outfit. First mount a brown triangle on a white background, dividing the page in half diagonally. Cut photo mats using decorative scissors. Layer cream paper on upper left portions of two blue heart die cuts (Accu-Cut). Outline and draw stitches on all die-cut edges. Adhere die cuts and stickers (NRN Designs, Frances Meyer). Write titles and captions.

When We Were One

Digging up old family photos helped Julie settle a family "feud" about which side of the family her son most resembled. For each photo, cut a tan and brown mat. Print and trace the Playbill font (Sierra On-Line) for the title words; double mat each word. Journal and write photo labels with black pen; mat with tan or brown.

historic photos & newspaper clippings

For an archival-quality album environment:

◆ Assume all memorabilia is acidic; never let photos and memorabilia touch.

◆ To preserve old newspaper clippings and announcements, spray with de-acidification spray (such as Archival Mist™ by Preservation Technologies) or photocopy the clippings onto oatmeal-colored paper (to preserve antique look) prior to mounting.

◆ Use only acid- and lignin-free paper, photo-safe adhesives and pigment inks.

◆ Handle photos with care; avoid direct light.

◆ Use nonpermanent mounting techniques (photo corners, sleeves, etc.) for easy removal for copying or restoration.

◆ Keep cropping to a minimum; background objects tell their own stories of place and time.

◆ Don't trim or hand-tint old photos. Have reprints made first.

I Think That I Shall Never See . . .

An old illustration of a ship helps link contemporary photos of MaryJo's sailor-suited sons to their ancestors' voyage to America. Begin with a navy background (Canson); add ¼" strips of gold paper at top and bottom. Photocopy clip art on cream paper; mount. Add navy-colored oval trimmed with deckle scissors above ship. Journal on vellum; trim with deckle scissors and adhere. Oval crop photos; adhere. Adhere matted title at top and bottom of page. Finish with embellishments (Creative Beginnings).

I think that
I shall never see...

Grandpa 'Boppa' Don Regier 3 months, 1933

Dylan, 3 months, 1989

Jacob, 3 months, 1992

-whose ancestors came to America
from Southern Russia in 1879-

Colt, 3 months, 1986

Hunter, 3 months, 1990

Four grandsons who
look more like me!

Three Generations

Efrat's hand-tinted photos and museum-like framing of three generations of the Cain family is reminiscent of yesteryear. Use striped paper (The Family Archives) for background "wallpaper." Triple mat photos with gold, cream and burgundy papers. Layer gold frame (Sonburn) over photos. Finish with matted journaling and gold ribbon.

Precious Legacy

1928
Harold Eugene Cain

1955
Harold Joe Cain

1981
John Harold Cain

Three Generations

projects

sleepytime

Nothing's as sweet as a slumbering baby. Capture these moments on film and record how you achieved them. Was it the blankie's satin edge that did the trick? A soothing lullaby? The security of falling off to sleep is a memory you will cherish and your baby will carry in his heart forever.

Twinkle Little Star

The stamps provided Cathy's design idea. To make the border, stamp and emboss blue dots and dashes, blue crescent moons and yellow stars (Stampin' Up!). Color stars and moons yellow and baby clothes blue. Cut large crescent moon and baby blanket from printed paper (The Paper Patch); layer with silhouetted photo. Add dimension to moon and blanket edges with Liquid Appliqué (Marvy Uchida). Adhere ribbon bows. Write titles in yellow.

Sleeping Baby Quilt

Jessica's photos lend the perfect focus to a baby quilt. Start by mounting photos in desired positions. Fill white spaces with colored and printed paper (Provo Craft) strips. Cut heart, star, flower and duck shapes. Punch ¼" circle for flower center. Finish with pen stroke stitching.

A Little Bird Told Me . . .

Barbara crafted this Geddes-style page for her granddaughter's birthday. Print the lettering and clip art bird directly on lavender background paper. Color bird. Freehand cut nest shape, trimming top edges with large oak leaf punch. Crumple thin brown strips. Layer photo and nest pieces with punched oak leaves and vine die cut (Ellison). Journal and draw details with black pen.

The Story of Pooh and Twin

When Cindy bought her son a "spare" Pooh as a backup, he soon needed both to sleep. For the page background, use yellow printed paper (Keeping Memories Alive). Double mat photos with soft blue solid and printed paper (Keeping Memories Alive). Cut soft blue mat for journaling. Punch Pooh bears (All Night Media) along the bottom of the mat. Write title, using the punched shapes for the "O" letters in "Pooh." Adhere Pooh stickers (Michel & Co.).

a little bird told me
there's someone new in
the nest.....

...Jessica Lynn...

...June 15, 1991

The Story
of
Pooh &
Twin

Austen got his Pooh bear from Nana at his baby shower. He had become so attached to Pooh that we had to buy a spare. No store had them anymore so I logged on to the Internet to see if the company could find me to a store that carried it. They did and we bought TWIN. Now Austen is attached to BOTH bears and needs both to sleep. He loves his Poohs.

UP ALL NIGHT

Most of all the other beautiful things in life come by twos and threes, by dozens and hundreds. Plenty of roses, stars, sunsets, rainbows, brothers and sisters, aunts and cousins, but only one mother in the whole world. *Kate Douglas Wiggin*

Mommy and Justin June 1999

For Baby (For Bobbie)
By John Denver

This is one of Mommy's favorite songs, and one that would calm you down when you cried.

Babies Smile in their Sleep because they are listening to the Whispering of Angels

Hannah June Irvine

Up All Night

Susan recorded that unforgettable part of new mother-hood-sleep deprivation. The pictures tell the story, so keep them the focal point with simple shapes and mats. For the window, freehand cut moon, curtain rod and curtains; layer with white strips on star paper (Creative Memories). Adhere letter stickers (Creative Memories) for title; accent with black dots. Journal with thick black pen.

Mommy's Favorite Lullaby

Sleeping baby pictures illustrate John Denver's "For Baby," a song that often calmed Stacey's daughter. For the background, mount gold and purple triangles in lower left and upper right corners. Print song lyrics and double mat with orange and star/moon printed paper (Colors by DESIGN). Crop and mat diamond shape for journaling and star and oval photos. Punch small stars and moons.

Special Delivery

Matching borders tie Kathi's theme page to her portrait page. For the page borders, draw scalloped lines using a thick purple pen. For the portrait, trim photo corners using a corner lace punch (McGill) and mount on printed clip art frame. Layer strips of printed quilt clip art around edges. Trim photo in envelope using corner heart punch (McGill). For stamps, cut and mat small photos, printed title, and printed clip art; trim mats with stamp scissors (Fiskars). For mailbox, print clip art and layer with silhouetted photo. Adhere small punched heart and floral clip art. Journal with black pen. (All clip art from Microsoft's® Greetings Workshop CD.)

Mason Garret Collins

To customize a baby gift page made for Mason's mother, Donna photocopied Mason's great-great-great-grandmother's quilt for background. Note that baby is sleeping on quilt in photo, too. To make the photo frame, quadruple mat with red, white and mulberry paper. Print title and trim with deckle scissors; mat with red paper. Adhere red ribbon bow.

Quilling

Quilling, an ancient art originally known as paper filigree, involves rolling thin strips of paper into various shapes and arranging those shapes into a design. Perhaps you made quilled art as a child. Quilling supplies are quite inexpensive and as you can see, quilling adds a fun and playful touch to baby scrapbook pages. The standard width of quilling paper is ⅛", but wider and narrower sizes are available. Besides quilling paper (Lake City Craft Quilling Supplies), you'll need glue and a slotted or needle tool. Rolling paper around the tool makes various shapes, while the number of coils made determines the thickness of the shape.

how to roll quill shapes with a needle tool

1. Cut off a strip of paper to the desired length.
2. Slide paper strip into slot of tool and press the end of the paper around the tool with your thumb.
3. Roll the paper while holding the tool steady, keeping the strip's edges as even as possible (Figure 1).
4. Pinch ends, as needed (Figure 2).
5. Glue shapes together (Figure 3); adhere to page.

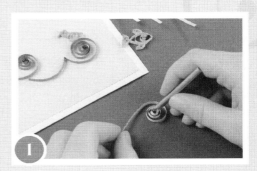

how to roll various shapes

Loose Scrolls Roll one end, leaving the other end loose.

Loose Circles Roll, remove from tool and let the coil loosen. Glue the loose end.

Teardrops Roll and glue a loose circle. Pinch one side of the circle to a point.

Marquise Roll and glue a loose circle. Pinch on both ends.

Tight Circles Roll, slip the tool from the roll's center and hold it to keep it from unwinding. Glue the loose end of the paper to the side of the roll.

I'm bringing home my girlfriend to meet my Mom and Dad. We'll laugh and have a good time, but then it will turn bad, when Mom gets out the Scrapbook when I was "oh

The Girlfriend Page

...so cute" and that first page that she will show is me in my Birthday Suit!

BY MOMMY

The Girlfriend (or Boyfriend) Page

No baby album is complete without an adorable "blackmail" page!

Concept/Poem by Gina Emerson
Salisbury, North Carolina

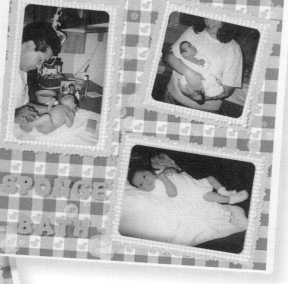

Olivia's First Sponge Bath

Craft foam matched the sponge-bath theme of Tracy's fun layout. Start with duck printed paper (The Paper Patch) for page background. Round corners of photos, double mat using decorative scissors and gingham and polka dot paper. Trace title letters (Pebbles In My Pocket) onto craft foam and cut out. Mat yellow gingham duck die cut (Creative Memories); cut foam beak, black eye and wing detail. For bubbles, punch and layer different sizes of vellum circles, highlighting with white and blue markers.

Bathtime

Nancy cut checkerboard paper into square tiles to mimic her parents' 1940s bathroom. Start with a green background. Cut and mat circle photos and "bubble" for title. Cut white strips for chair railing and windowpane. Arrange squares of checkerboard paper for tile pattern. Cut pieces for bathtub, tub feet and window. Layer photo and stickers (Stickopotamus) beneath tub. Adhere additional stickers.

Bathtime

The gray grout lines give Jacqueline's page a bathtub backdrop. After drawing the gray lines, cut faucet handles, spout and water droplet. Write title with thick and thin blue pens. Circle cut and silhouette photos. Layer photos with bubble stickers (Frances Meyer), duck die cuts (Creative Memories) and blue and white circles. Color ducks' beaks orange. Draw details with blue and black pens.

Bathtime Pop-up

Pop-up pages are full of surprises, magic and fun. And best of all, making pop-ups is easier than you might think!

1. Use a white 12" × 12" scrapbook page for background. Silhouette cut large bubble paper (Hot Off The Press); adhere to lower left corner of page.

2. Sandwich together one 8½" × 11" sheet of large bubble paper and one 8½" × 11" sheet of small bubble paper (Hot Off The Press) with right sides out; glue. Repeat with a second set of large and small bubble paper. Silhouette cut each bubble paper "sandwich." Layer together and adhere top of bubble papers to top ⅓ of background page. Fold up bottom ⅔ of bubble paper to form lift-up flap.

3. Transfer pattern on page 72 and center it on an 8½" × 11" sheet of white card stock. Fold card on fold line; cut on dotted lines (Figure 1).

4. Open card and carefully push out on the strips created to form the pop-ups (Figure 2).

5. Cover top half of pop-up with striped paper (NRN Designs) for "wallpaper" and bottom half with quilted paper (The Paper Patch) for "linoleum," trimming where needed to accommodate pop-up flaps (Figure 3). Lift up bubble paper flap and mount pop-up card to page.

6. Freehand cut bathtub and sink. Silhouette crop photos for bathtub; adhere to bathtub and add bubble stickers. Mount on pop-up strips (Figure 4). Add toiletry stickers (Mrs. Grossman's, Stickopotamus), placing foam spacers under bathroom scale, soap and some bubbles for added dimension. Trim a piece of old washcloth with fancy scissors for floor mat; adhere. If desired, make "puddles" on floor by using two coats of thick, clear embossing enamel.

7. Silhouette cut photos for front of pop-up card. Adhere to front of pop-up card, tucking under silhouetted bubbles where needed. Journal front of pop-up to complete.

Grandma's Brag Book

Becky's mother lives 12 hours away, so when her first grandchild was born, Becky shared the moments in a "Grandma's Brag book" theme album. The expandable album (Creative Memories) allows Becky to send her mother pages to "keep Grandma updated" on Baby's growth and activities. And even though the color theme varies from page to page, simple page treatments give the book its consistent look.

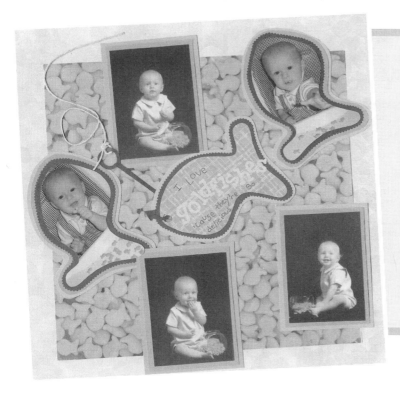

I Love Goldfish

To match the theme of the portraits, Michelle color copied crackers in a plastic bag. Start by layering photocopied paper on a blue printed background (Provo Craft). Double mat portraits. Crop snapshots and orange paper into fish shapes; double or triple mat, trimming the black mats with decorative scissors. Write title and adhere letter stickers (Frances Meyer). Freehand cut hook and put through punched hole. Tie twine around the fishhook eye.

Too Pooped to Eat

Rather than wake a sleeping baby, Michelle's husband made a pillow for their sleeping son. Use striped paper (Keeping Memories Alive) for background. Mat photos with white, checkerboard and printed paper (Keeping Memories Alive); trim yellow mats with fancy scissors. Cut title letters with template (Frances Meyer). Punch large white flowers and small yellow circles for centers. Freehand cut white flower and large yellow circle, journal and draw details.

Chicken Pox

A coloring book helped Bonita design this poor sick character. Start by rounding corners of photos and mats; layer on navy background. Draw and mat "fever" style title using thermometers in some of the letters. Cut and layer pieces for sick giraffe using printed paper (Paper Parade) for body. Draw details with colored pens.

Emergency

Cathy tucked get-well cards from her daughter's 1971 bout with croup into this medical-theme pocket page. For the top border, adhere line, letter and hospital-theme stickers (Creative Memories, Frances Meyer). For the pocket, cut a rectangle about half the size of the page and adhere along left, bottom and right sides. To decorate the pocket, mount polka dot paper along with a strip of white paper trimmed with decorative scissors. Outline with border stickers. Accent page with additional stickers and black dots.

Memory Wheel

Memory wheels are easily adaptable to scrapbook pages and are great space savers, using five photos at a time.

1. Cut two 10½" circle "wheels." Glue together for strength. Trim outer edge with zigzag scissors for firm grip when turning wheel. Insert brad fastener through center of wheel and attach to center of background page (Figure 1). Spin wheel to ensure that it spins freely on page.

2. Cut five horizontal photos using photo pattern on page 72, positioning narrow part of pattern at bottom of photo subject. Mount photos securely on wheel with narrow bottoms surrounding center of wheel (Figure 2).

3. Use window pattern on page 72 to cut window opening 1½" down at center of cover paper that will cover the entire wheel. Place window opening over wheel, centering one photo in the window.

4. Lay window cover over mounted background and wheel; line up all edges. Use slot pattern on page 72 to mark slot for wheel on window cover paper over edge of wheel, underneath and 1" from page edge (Figure 3). Slot should point to left if wheel will turn on left side of page, right if wheel turns on right side of page. Remove window cover; cut open slot.

5. Place cover on background; slide edge of wheel through curved slot (Figure 4). Adhere cover to background at corners and edges, without capturing any of the wheel. Journal about the wheel's photos; decorate as desired.

Our Little Olympian

Inspired by the winter Olympics, Lesli posed these cute photos for different events. Cut two blue wavy strips and a 1¾" gold circle for medal. Mat photos and printed journaling; adhere. Add journaling and pen stroke stitching to medallion.

bobsled

weight lifting

sumo wrestling

our little olympian

rings

Chitchi's Story

New parents often marvel at the accomplishments of their off-spring. Each "first" is greeted with thoughts of the genius we have produced. The same is true for Chitchi and Louis and their son David. But one activity worried them a bit at first.

"David would crawl away to amuse himself, and we would find him with a line of objects stretching across the floor," says Chitchi. "We asked ourselves, 'What is he doing that for?'" Other parents whose children exhibited similar talents later reassured them. "We've come to realize that it's normal, especially for boys," says Chitchi.

Some of David's favorite items to line up are CDs, books, magnetic letters, placemats, shoes and cars. David will often call his line of books his "train."

"He really takes after his dad's organizational skills," says Chitchi. "David has always put his toys away without being asked."

David has recently graduated to a higher level of organization. Previously he would line up all of mom's punches, regardless of size or shape. Now he sorts punches into distinct lines, separating the border, mini and jumbo tools into their own paths.

David doesn't line up things as often anymore, which makes Chitchi glad she documented his efforts on a special scrapbook page.

Get in line! And see how our son David would line things up like a pro! Ever since David was about 15 months, we would often walk into a room and find all the books laid out on the floor, lined up from one wall to the other! We can't explain why he does this but it's sure fun to watch him do it. And don't you dare take any of the objects out of formation, David is pretty serious about this job of his!!!

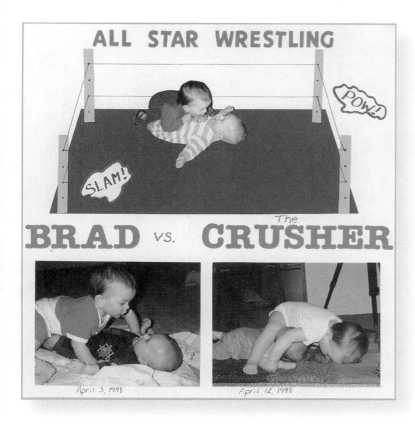

Brad vs. Crusher

Patti's humorous page captures the times her older son tried to show little brother who was boss. For the wrestling ring, cut navy mat and tan poles. Draw lines to enclose the ring. Cut free form white pieces for the words "slam" and "pow" and outline with thick black pen. Silhouette photo. Adhere small (Current) and large letter stickers (Creative Memories) for titles.

Next?

Liz scanned her son's pajamas to re-create the fabric's giraffe design. For the giraffe's spots, punch ⅛" and ¼" red circles; adhere. For title squares, stamp "Wasn't there, didn't do it" design (Rubber Monger), heat emboss and cut out. Mount giraffe and stamped squares. Punch ¹⁄₁₆" dots and mount around giraffe. Stamp title letters (Stampendous) in each square. Mat portrait with red paper and trim with jumbo deckle scissors (Family Treasures).

The Baby Patch

Cathie's embossed stamping highlights this berry-licious page. Use black paper for background; add ⅛" white paper border. Layer trimmed heart and matted checkered papers (The Paper Patch). Mat cropped photos; adhere. Stamp coneflowers (Mostly Animals), angels and fairies (Stamposaurus), sign (DJ Inkers), bunnies (Artistic Stamp Exchange) and berries (Sonlight). Emboss stamped designs; cut out and adhere.

So Many Names

Kris and her family had so many nicknames for her son that someone once commented that Samuel might never learn his name. The words are printed directly on the background paper. To do so, use a computer to print the title and different names using a variety of fonts. (The page shown uses two horizontally overlapping 8½" × 11" pages.) Position the names so that they fit around a silhouetted photo.

Peek-a-Boo Pie

Scrapbook artists are continually searching for creative ways to use more and more photos on one scrapbook page. The peek-a-boo pie technique is a fun and easy solution.

1. Mount berry paper (Frances Meyer) for background.

2. Cut one 11" circle (top crust) and one 10" circle (bottom crust) from tan card stock. Trim top crust using cloud scissors (Fiskars) to form pie's "scalloped" edge (Figure 1).

3. Transfer pie pattern on page 72 to top crust. Use a craft knife to carefully cut on all dotted lines (Figure 2). Scoring with a stylus will help create nice, crisp folds on flaps.

4. Adhere top crust to bottom crust; mount on background leaving enough room for page title.

5. Silhouette-cut six favorite photos and mount beneath flaps onto bottom pie crust (Figure 3). Journal about each photo on inside of pie flaps. Add title lettering.

The Dreaded Dust Bunny

When her little ones had too much fun with the baby powder, Michele decided it was a Kodak moment. Start by cutting ¾" gray strips and four 2½" gray squares. Cut squares in half diagonally. Stamp and emboss winter daisy border (Close to My Heart™/D.O.T.S.) on strips and triangles. Mount triangles in corners of parchment background. Layer strips around each photo. Print story; trim story edges with decorative scissors and mat with gray paper. Stamp, emboss and cut out bunnies. Color pink bunny ears and cheeks.

Even Angels Have Bad Days

When Renee's normally angelic son decided he didn't want to be Cupid for his first Valentine's Day birthday, she made the best of it as well as this adorable page. Cut the title using letter die cuts as templates. Mat main oval photo with white paper; trim with decorative scissors. Arrange with other oval photos on colored background; trim edges with decorative scissors. Write title and journaling. Adhere angel stickers (Creative Memories).

Aidan's 1st Shoes

Ellen cleverly traced around her son's shoes to help record his first steps. To make the path, diagonally piece 5½" light gray strips on a green background. Adhere grass stickers (Mrs. Grossman's) along edge of path. Freehand cut dark gray pebbles to fit on the path. Make a template from a baby shoe to crop the photos. Deckle trim brown photo mats. Tear and crumple brown paper for journaling to look like a piece of trash for the ants to carry away. Adhere ant stickers (Provo Craft).

My First Haircut

After five homemade haircuts, Kim took her son to the barbershop. To make the barber's pole borders, use a wavy ruler to draw parallel wavy lines about ½" apart on red and blue paper. Cut two blue and two red wavy strips. Intertwine a red and blue strip for each border. Cut gray rectangles for the tops and bottoms and connect with black lines. Crop and mat circle, oval and octagonal photos using decorative scissors. Place hair in memorabilia pocket (3L Corp.). Adhere haircut-theme stickers (Frances Meyer).

Meghan's Milestones

Sits up ~ 7 months

Cruises 8 months

Walks! 12 mos.

Pushes up ~ 5 months

Pulls up ~ 7 mos.

Lifts head ~ 3 months

Crawls 7 months

Rolls ~ 5½ mos.

Plays with feet

3-6 months

Meghan's Milestones

Ellen's "road to success" highlights her daughter's milestones from crawling to walking. White dots add even more dimension. To complete the background, cut a yellow sun, green grass and black road, layering as shown. Draw road and sun details with a yellow opaque marker. Cut gray stones and layer with silhouetted photos. Adhere flower (Mrs. Grossman's) and insect (Michel & Co.) stickers. Add title stickers (Making Memories); outline with white opaque pen. Journal and draw details.

page 28

page 30

page 31

page 25

Austen and Mommy
frolicking in the
beautiful sunshine.
Heritage Park
AUGUST 1998

page 33

too pooped to eat

page 49

father

October 1962

David Duane Lisenby

Son

November 1995

Andrew Butler Lisenby

Precious Legacy

1928
Harold Eugene Cain

1955
Harold Joe Cain

1981
John Harold Cain

Three Generations

my daddy does silly things with me

my daddy can touch his finger to the moon

He comforts me when I'm sick

Baby Girl

down through a field of stars & moonbeams, you were born into this world, and the happiness and blessed joy you bring to us is more radiant than the sun and older than the moon. The world belongs to you, Baby Kitty, along with all our love.

Kathryn Elizabeth Pittard

8 Months Old   June 8, 1997

It's a Boy

Baby Jussie Bear, our boy
born on the wings of hope and
dreams, you are overflowing with the
purity of innocence and all our
promises of tomorrow. The world
belongs to you and as you begin your
journey, always remember how
much we love you.

Triston
Michael
Pittard

8 Months Old   June 8, 1997

pages 64-65

page 56

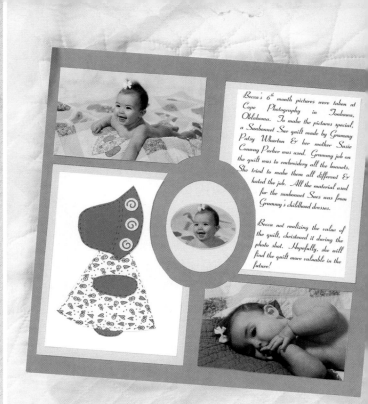

page 67

page 59

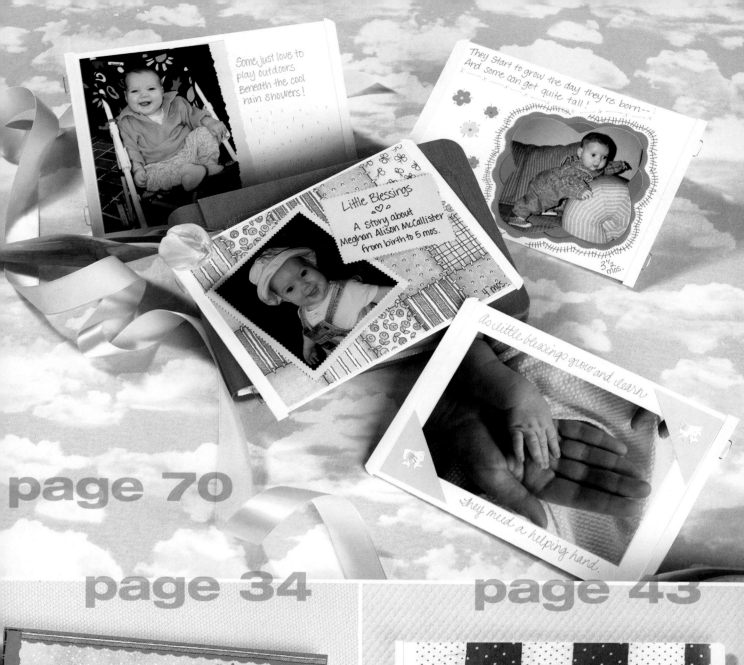

Some just love to
play outdoors
Beneath the cool
rain showers!

They start to grow the day they're born—
And some can get quite tall!

Little Blessings
♡♡
A story about
Meghan Alison McCallister
from birth to 5 mos.

4 mos.

3½ mos.

As little blessings grow and learn

They need a helping hand.

page 70

page 34

page 43

When all else fails…

Snuggle your
Daddy!

Mason Garret Collins
January 21, 1998 at 3:14 p.m.
7 pounds, 10 1/2 ounces   20 1/2 inches
"God blesses all the earth with the precious gift of children to bring us
warmth and sweetness, laughter and love."

step-by-step projects

CUTIE PIE

Bathtime

Buddies

Nice hairdo . . . you too!

Andrew at age 3 and Emily at age 1   August 22, 1980

ouch!

The Big Accident

TURN

Christine, Fred and Alexis were over because Fred was helping Daddy put up a fence in the backyard. You lost your balance and fell down the steps of the deck and knocked off a beer bottle as you were falling and landed on the broken glass. You cut your face and your leg. There was a lot of blood. The cut on your face was pretty big, it was opened up about one inch wide. Daddy said he wished we never saw it because we will never forget how horrible that wound looked! The ambulance came pretty quick and everyone was very helpful as we rushed you to the hospital. But on the way there, the ambulance had a car accident! A car cut off the ambulance and we hit it pretty hard, we all went flying and landed on top of fireman Frank Pistilli. Poor Frank, he hit the inside of the ambulance and was cut on his head and eye and had blood all over his face. Daddy hit his head and had a big bump and you and I were ok. So we had to wait for another ambulance and we finally got to the hospital.

At the hospital you had a catscan to check for any internal swelling and an x-ray to check for glass in the wounds. During the x-ray you asked "whats that?" and Daddy said "it's a big camera to take your picture".

So you thought about it and then said "CHEESE!" into the x-ray machine. The technicians thought you were adorable.

We have a friend at APC who is a plastic surgeon, Dr. Sid Rabinowitz, and he ended up being on call that night! We were so thankful, he was so nice which calmed us down a lot. Dr Sid decided that stitching you up in the operating room would be best. They worked on you for over an hour and you had over 100 stitches on your face! He stitched up the two cuts on your leg too. It was midnight when you finally got into your room and you stayed over night with Mommy sleeping right next to you. When we finally saw your scar, we couldn't believe the difference! Dr. Sid did a great job! Now we put lots of sunblock on it and medicine and wait to see if the scar will fade.

So many friends and family sent you gifts, cards and balloons too. You got many new toys, puzzles and books.

Whenever you saw the scar on your leg you would kiss it and say "all better". And when you saw your face in a mirror you would ask "you gotta booboo?" And Mommy would say "yes, but it is all better now" and it is!

SWINGING IN THE SUMMER BREEZE BARE TOES AND CHUBBY KNEES. BRANDON JULY 1998

First Airplane Ride

Bamber's page commemorates not only moving from Paris to the United States, but also surviving an international plane ride with an infant. Start by mounting photos and airplane die cut (Creative Memories). Print title letters in an open faced font. Cut out title letters, mat with blue, and color in yellow. Adhere airplane stickers (Mrs. Grossman's).

The Baby Boy Who Could

Jennifer built the photo mountain by piecing photos together and cutting the top edge. For the train track, layer small brown rectangles on a thick black line. Silhouette photos and layer with the train die cuts (Ellison) along with black and colored circles and strips. Cut various sizes of light blue clouds. Adhere letter stickers (Frances Meyer) for the title and journal with black pen.

Growth Spurt

Circle photos and just two paper colors keeps Linda's layout simple to document progress. To make the title, adhere letter (Creative Memories) and toy (Hallmark) stickers to white paper strip; mat with light green paper. Crop and mat photos. Print, cut out and mat growth chart and photo labels. Arrange elements on page with rattle die cut (Creative Memories). Accent with additional toy stickers.

Watch Me Grow

Mary labeled her pictures by putting a sign in each monthly photo. Use bear and swirl printed paper (Design Originals) for background. Round corners of photos; mat and adhere. Print title using the Market font (Microsoft). Adhere die cuts (Colorbök).

Aidan's Teeth

Ellen scanned the tooth chart from a baby book and changed the colors to match her page. To complete the chart, deckle cut black and white mats and cut a pink oval for the center. For the border, cut pink gums with a scallop ruler and round corners of white rectangles for teeth. Circle cut photos. Double mat the larger photos with white and pink, trimming the white mats with notch scissors (Fiskars). Draw and mat title and adhere toothbrush and toothpaste stickers (Mrs. Grossman's). Journal on the dental chart and write photo captions. Layer page elements on a black background.

baby's milestone memories

Your baby's infancy will be packed with important "firsts." While it may sound like a lot of work to photograph and record these incidents, you will never regret it. Be on the lookout for the following milestones to enhance your baby's scrapbook album:

- Clapping
- Crawling
- Drinking from cup
- First bath
- First birthday
- First haircut

- First holidays
- First illness
- First laugh
- First outing
- First smile
- First solid food

- First steps
- First tooth
- First words
- Lifts head
- Pulls self up
- Reaches for objects

- Rolls over
- Sits up
- Stands
- Waves

projects

One to Twelve Months

Linda's journaling style is a quick way to cover a year's progress. Start by dividing the page into twelve equal boxes using a ruler and thick black pen. Crop and mount photos. Write month titles. Adhere star stickers (Mrs. Grossman's) and journal about each month's milestones.

butterfly baby

To turn your baby into a butterfly, silhouette photo; add hand cut wings and antennae.

Calendar Girl

These pages are part of a four-page layout Kathryn displays using panoramic page protectors. For the title, adhere letter stickers (Making Memories) on gray background. Layer quilt design using square photos and colored and printed strips and shapes. For bunny (Design Originals Punchin'), punch medium and small gray hearts. Cut hearts in half for ears, feet and hands. Punch mini red hearts for tongue and nose. Accent each bunny with a monthly or seasonal theme using additional punches or cut-shapes. Journal and draw details and outlines with black pen.

Baby Girl

down through a field of stars & moonbeams, you were born into this world and the happiness and blessed joy you bring to us is more radiant than the sun and older than the moon. The world belongs to you Baby Kitty, along with all our love.

Kathryn Elizabeth Pittard

8 Months Old · June 8, 1997

It's a Boy & Baby Girl

Stickers with a clear background (me & my BIG ideas) make Donna's pages look like custom printed paper. First mount each portrait on a colored background. Journal with silver and highlight with white. Outline page titles with silver and fill in with white. Trim and adhere stickers around portrait, borders and titles.

Photo Kaleidoscope Mats

Photo kaleidoscope mats allow you to showcase cherished baby photos or create highly personalized gifts. For a polished look, the photo kaleidoscope mat should be created using a photo with colors that complement the center photo.

Making a photo kaleidoscope mat is easier than you might think, as you will see in the steps below. To learn more on creating photo kaleidoscopes, see *Memory Makers Photo Kaleidoscopes*™.

1. Select the photo you will use to create the photo kaleidoscope mat; have four original 4" × 6" duplicate photos and four reverse 4" × 6" photos made (Figure 1).

2. Using one original print, place the longest edge of a 45° triangle along the 6" side of the photo with the triangle point meeting a corner of the photo; mark the cutting line (Figure 2). Repeat with the remaining three original photos.

3. Layer one original cut photo on top of one reverse uncut photo and tape together at matching corners to create a mirror image. Place ruler over photo; cut on reverse photo. Now you have one pair (Figure 3). Repeat with remaining uncut three reverse photos to make three more pairs.

4. When finished cutting, mount all pairs onto page. Place another selected photo or artwork in the center and then frame as desired.

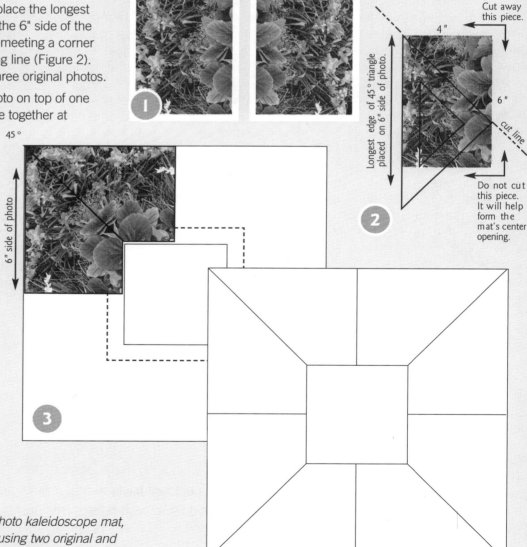

Note: To make an 8" × 10" photo kaleidoscope mat, follow the instructions above using two original and two reversed-image 4" × 6" photos.

Becca

The Sunbonnet Sue design ties in the baby quilt made especially for this portrait of Robyn's daughter. First cut a small oval photo for the page center. Print journaling, adjusting the margins as necessary. Mat the journaling and a similar size white rectangle. Use an oval template (Puzzle Mates) to cut the center oval mat and trim the surrounding elements. Cut pieces for Sunbonnet Sue using printed (Provo Craft) and cranberry paper. To decorate the bonnet, punch small yellow circles and mini cranberry swirls. Draw details with black pen.

Portrait Storybook Album

Julie combined professional portraits and candid photos of her daughter Katie into a storybook. Punch art and stickers, along with the simple captioning and photo matting, give her little album its clean, crisp appearance. "Katie loves to read her album because the story and pictures are all about her," says Julie.

Paper Folding

Paper folding is a fun and unique way to embellish your scrapbook pages. With a few folds here, a few tucks there and some creative assembly, you can frame your photos with paper art that is reminiscent of ancient origami. And it's easy to do.

There are many different folds you can use. Here we feature the pointed petal corner fold. It's a great fold to use for experimenting with paper positioning. By assembling folded pieces in a ring, you can create a round frame. Altering the number of folded pieces and the assembly method can yield square frames or smaller wreaths, with no openings, to use as embellishments.

For the wreath shown here, you'll need twenty-five 2½" squares (twenty-one for the frame and four for the corners) of lightweight denim paper (Hot Off The Press). One 8½" × 11" paper will yield twelve squares. Fold each piece following the steps below. Try folding a practice piece first.

pointed petal corner fold

1. With pattern side facing up, fold C and D to A and B and crease.
2. Open flat, fold A and C to B and D and crease.
3. Open flat and turn paper over with pattern side down.
4. Bring A to D, forming a triangle and crease.
5. Open flat, fold C to B, forming a triangle and crease.
6. Holding folded corners in either hand, push fingers toward center, as shown. Move the flap in your left hand toward the back and bring flap in your right hand forward, forming a layered triangle.
7. Bring top right flap to left side.
8. Fold top left flap down along centerline and crease.
9. Slide finger between remaining left flaps.
10. Bring top left flap to right side.
11. Fold top right flap down along centerline and crease.
12. Bring top right flap to left side.

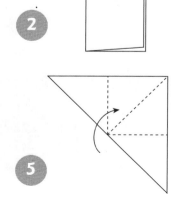

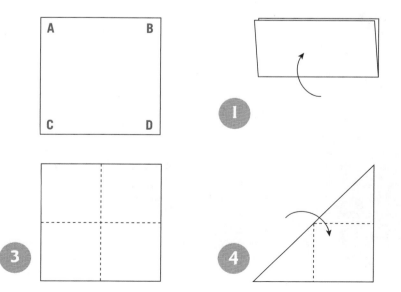

assembly

◆ Line up twenty-one pieces on circle's edge with even spacing and using the same reference points on each folded paper as shown.

◆ Holding two pieces with closed points facing same direction, place flap of one piece into space between flap and diamond of the other.

◆ Snug up pieces so that the long open end of inserted piece is flush with edge of diamond of other piece.

◆ Secure with adhesive.

◆ Repeat remaining pieces, sliding first piece into last to finish.

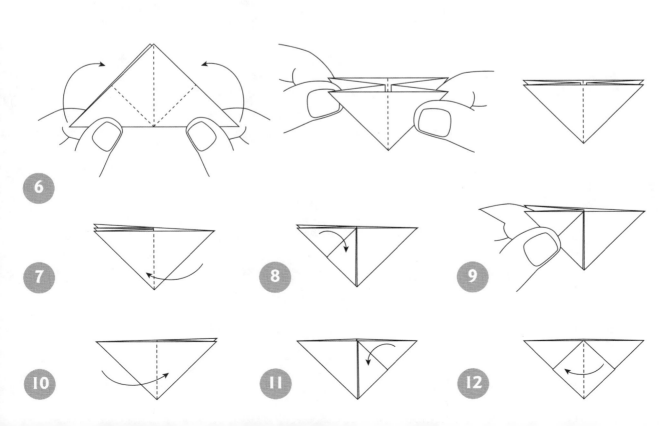

6

7

8

9

10

11

12

Some just love to
play outdoors
Beneath the cool
rain showers!

They start to grow the day they're born--
And some can get quite tall!

Little Blessings
A story about
Meghan Alison McCallister
from birth to 5 mos.

3½ mos.

4 mos.

As little blessings grow and learn

They need a helping hand.

Little Blessings Storybook Album

In three days, Melissa made four of these charming "Little Blessings" books for relatives as Christmas gifts. The book's theme, based on a Precious Moments™ book titled *Little Blessings*, helps share baby's good times with someone dear. The album's photos convey the story of Meghan's first five months for grandparents and great-grandparents who might have otherwise missed out on her joyful, daily growth. Note how the simple page treatments and captioning help draw attention to the baby's photos. "The storybooks were a big hit on Christmas day!" says Melissa.

Pop-Up, Pull-Out Storybook Album

Susan turned her granddaughter Bailey's love of books into a storybook for Baily. The album is full of little pop-up, pull-out, slide, peek-a-boo and wheel pages, always an entertaining favorite of young children. The album's high-energy colors work well with photos of busy Bailey. Also included are photos of grandparents and other relatives. "I wanted her to be able to see us when we can't be around," says Susan.

projects

patterns
Use these helpful patterns to complete certain scrapbook pages featured in this book. Photocopy and enlarge as needed.

Peek-a-Boo Pie

Pie pattern for Peek-a-Boo Pie, page 55. Enlarge to 224% on a photocopier for a 12" x 15" page, 163% for a 8½" x 11" page.

Memory Wheel

Photo pattern for Memory Wheel, page 51. Enlarge on a photocopier to 167%.

Slot pattern for Memory Wheel, page 51. Enlarge on a photocopier to 167%.

Window pattern for Memory Wheel, page 51. Enlarge on a photocopier to 167%.

Bathtime Pop-up

Pop-up pattern for Bathtime Pop-up, page 47. Enlarge on a photocopier to 140%.

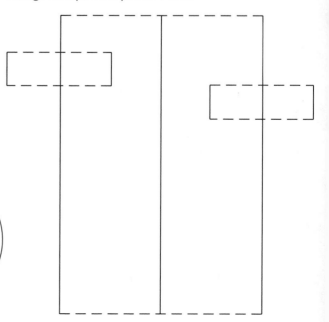

Appendix

Example Scrapbook

Lettering Alphabets

Bow Tie

If a scrapbook page is a wrapped present, then this flowing cursive alphabet is the ribbon. You can almost imagine curling different lengths into each casually elegant letter. The widened points even mimic the snipped ends of a pretty bow.

Although it looks fancy, this script is easy to master because it doesn't require perfection. You can replicate the feel of each letter without having to copy exactly. Starting with penciled guidelines, draw the basic shape of each letter. Connect letters if it seems natural, such as the letter m flowing into the letter a. If the connection seems awkward, as in the letter w followed by the letter e, just end the first letter and start the next one beside it.

When you're happy with the overall flow of each word, add extra swirls and curves where needed. The transitions from thin lines to thick are an important element in this lettering, so be sure to outline the thicker parts of each letter. Note that all lines in this alphabet are curved except for the widened letter ends, which are blunt.

Now it's time to color. Dress up this style with a metallic pen on dark paper, or go more casual with bright colors. Add fancy embellishments or let the letters stand alone. Whatever your preference, this beautiful script is versatile enough for almost any purpose.

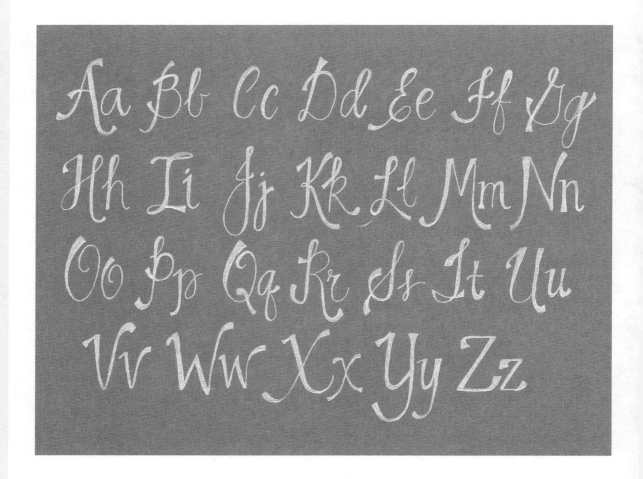

Fluffy

Write the alphabet using your fanciest printing. Then write it again with your best cursive. Now choose the characters from each set that you like the best. What do you get? The handwriting you've always wanted—a sophisticated cross between fancy printed and cursive characters.

This lettering requires consistent heights and even lines, so be sure to pencil guidelines before you start. After lightly drawing each letter, decide whether you want any characters to be connected as in a cursive style. Then draw the connecting lines. When you're satisfied, trace each letter with a medium to thick pen. The pen tip should be uniform because the lines in each character are the same width and don't vary.

To fully master this style takes some practice. Start out by tracing it several times on inexpensive ruled notebook paper. Once you get the feel for each character, try drawing words freehand. You'll be glad you invested the time because Fluffy is a terrific look to add to your repertoire of lettering styles for both captions and titles.

ABCDEFG
HIJKLM
NOPQRST
UVWXYZ

abcdefghi
jklmnopqr
stuvwxyz
1234567890

Debbie and Sande

BEST FRIENDS

· My Best Friend ·
We share many things
there is lots of laughter
and sometimes tears
as our days together
turn into years.

mom and PERRY COMO

Now—More Dates—More Fun!

How Barbra Whittemore made herself over at home, became a Campus Cinderella

"I was the loneliest of all people," says Barbra Whittemore, of East Lansing, Michigan, "a fat girl in a college town. My life was a social black-out." Then Barbra, like more than 300,000 other women and girls, enrolled in the DuBarry Success Course. Today, she's a slim, trim beauty—poised, sparkling. She acquired a smooth, lovely skin, learned to style her hair becomingly. And her social life? Invitations galore! The college boys call her Cinderella.

"I have so much more fun," says Barbra. The Success Course was worth its cost ten times over.

In the winter of 1946, my mom, Barbra Whittemore, won a contest after participating in the DuBarry Success Course. She won a brand new wardrobe and a trip to New York to do some modeling and to meet Perry Como. She also appeared in the February 10, 1947 issue of Life Magazine.

Coincidental Cousins

MELANIE

On the night of April 4, 1997, Laura was induced because she had Toxemia. I went to be with her at Presbyterian St. Lukes hospital in Denver. Well, April 4th was my due date... at 11:30 p.m. Laura's doctor sent us all home to wait until morning. On the way home my labor started... what a coincidence! Melanie Rose DiMinno was born at 12:30 a.m. on April 5th, 1997 and Delaney Kate Womack was born at 5:54 a.m. on April 5th, 1997 across the street from her cousin at St. Joseph's Hospital in Denver, Colorado.

Melanie

Delaney

Elementary

Do you remember learning to print? Lips pressed together in concentration, eyes focused on blue rule lines and a small fist squeezing a freshly sharpened #2 pencil, you carefully tried to copy perfectly printed letters. The result was always less than perfect but reflected your individuality. Elementary lettering captures this charming personality.

Unlike grade-school printing, this style is deliberately imperfect. The letters only loosely follow guidelines. Vertical and diagonal lines start and stop at different heights, avoiding that too-straight look. Not all loops are closed, as in the letters B and O, suggesting that the characters were written quickly.

And just to add to the cuteness, the letters g and y have sweet little loops.

You really can't make a mistake with this style if you're able to leave your perfectionist tendencies behind. Draw guidelines only if you want the letters to casually line up. Then pencil each character and trace with the pen color and thickness of your choice.

Use this lettering as a starting point for creating your own personal style of printing. Customize each letter with little idiosyncrasies that make it your own. The greater the imperfection, the greater the charm!

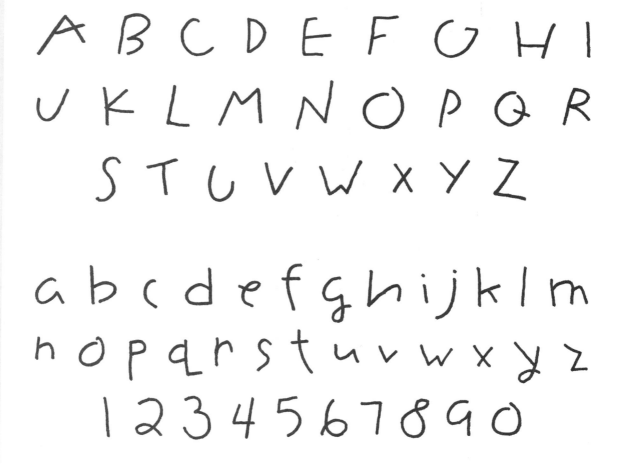

November 2:0:0:! 5th Grade

Young Ameritowne

The fifth grade students of Stony Creek Elementary ran a city for a day... they made the laws and elected a mayor and a towne sheriff. Dillon was chosen to be the manager accountant of the television station.

NEWS 4

NEWS 4 Colorado's News Channel

School Days

Dream

Barefoot Beauty

Signature

It's the contemporary yet classic cursive handwriting you've always dreamed of. Confident lines, smooth curves, simple flourishes. Before you say, "I can't write like that," give it a try. With some lined paper and a little practice, you'll soon be the envy of your scrapbooking friends.

To get the feel of each letter, lay ruled notebook paper over a photocopy of the letters and trace each character. Use the lines as a guide to keep the letters a consistent height. Draw each letter until you feel comfortable with its shape. You may notice that this style draws its contemporary as well as classic feel from the combination of mostly printed uppercase letters with cursive lowercase letters.

Now practice words and phrases, starting with your name and short titles. Note that while the uppercase letters are often unconnected, the lowercase letters are usually joined, whether directly or by gently touching edges. Lowercase letters may be unconnected when the first letter ends low and the second letter starts high, as in the word "an." Rather than relying on rigid rules to determine which letters should connect, focus on the overall visual flow, striving for movement throughout the word.

A B C D E F G H I
J K L M N O P Q R
S T U V W X Y Z

a b c d e f g h i j
k l m n o p q r s
t u v w x y z
1 2 3 4 5 6 7 8 9 0

When in Rome...
Amy and Joey · Spring 1984

The Pantheon
The Pantheon was built in 27 bc by Marcus Agrippa and reconstructed by Hadrian in the early 2nd century AD. It is probably the most reconsidered of all of Rome's buildings.

The Spanish Steps
The square from which the Spanish Steps lie, takes its name from the Spanish Embassy which used to have its headquarters here. It is a favorite meeting place.

The Trevi Fountain
Made famous in the film Three Coins in the Fountain. Tradition says if you throw a coin in it you will return. It is a masterpiece that was dated back to ancient Rome.

...do as the Romans do!

The Colosseum
Emperor Vespasian began building it in 70 AD and his son Titus completed it in 80 AD. At the height of the Colosseum could seat 50,000. It is still regarded as the greatest architectural masterpiece from ancient Rome.

Falling

DILLON AND DELANEY'S FAVORITE FALL TRADITION - DADDY RAKES THE LEAVES INTO A HUGE PILE - THE KIDS PLAY A WHILE AND THEN DADDY ENDS THE DAY TAKING PICTURES - 2001

for Fall

Pinstripe

Who says that pinstripes are just for men's fashion? They perfectly "suit" these contemporary, masculine letters, resulting in a tailored style that emphasizes vertical lines.

Start with guidelines to keep your letter heights even. Then pencil the basic letter shapes with single lines. Outline the wider parts of each character by drawing additional lines on either side of your base lines. If the line is straight, then the outlines should be straight and squared off at the top, as in the letter H. If the line curves, then the outlines should narrow and blend into the curve as it turns horizontal, as in the letter C. When a letter does not have

a vertical line, such as the letter X, then widen one diagonal line and leave the other line single. Note how the inside lines became the pinstriped.

A few sketching notes: Most of the uppercase characters are the same height except Y, which drops down below the baseline. Also, for variety, the lowercase g and j drop down lower than p and q.

The fun part is deciding how to colorize your letters. Consider black outlines and colored pinstripes, leaving the fill-in areas empty. Or draw all lines black and color the fill-in areas. Whatever you choose, you'll like the clean, crisp look of a well-tailored suit.

ABCDEFGHIJKLMN

OPQRSTUVWXYZ

1234567890

abcdefghijklmn

opqrstuvwxyz

They Say It's Your Birthday

Happy 30th To You

Amy

CHINA BUSINESS TRIP

...NGZHOU

I WENT TO CHINA IN APRIL OF 2000. I WENT WITH MY CLIENT, VIKKI, TO THE CANTON FAIRE IN THE CITY OF GUANGZHOU AND THE HONG KONG GIFT SHOW. IT WAS A FABULOUS TIME.

Hong Kong

Annual Christmas Card

We laughed, we made faces...and one at a time, we took our turn ruining the picture! 2 rolls of film and 48 pictures later... we got a decent one!

Family Photo Session

Dad!

Mom!

Dillon!

Delaney!

simple joys 2001
Jim, Sande, Dillon and Delaney

UNWRAP THE SMILES!

delaney
Christmas Morning · 2001

Sampler

The needle arts provide a wealth of ideas for creative scrapbookers. Quilting, appliqué, and cross-stitch patterns, among others, can be easily adapted for scrapbook designs. The same holds true for needle-point alphabets. This traditional lettering, inspired by the look of hand-stitched letters, yields the same effect without a needle and thread.

When arranging these letters, it's helpful to use graph paper as a grid, similar to a cross-stitch pattern. You can pencil a grid directly on paper or place graph paper on a light box so the grid shows through. The grid ensures uniform letter heights and spacing and makes it easy to draw diagonals. To determine the size of the grid, decide how wide you want the thicker parts of each letter. Make the grid the same size. If, for example, you want the line width to be ¼", use a ¼" grid.

Begin by outlining the thickest part of each letter. Then draw the thin lines, ending with the curved embellishments. Note that the thin lines may be straight and diagonal, as in the letter M, or more curved, as in the letter A.

When you're satisfied with the letters, color the outlines and fill with either a matching or contrasting color. Although this lettering style has a traditional look, you don't have to use conventional scrapbook supplies to create it. How about fabric and embroidery floss?

ABCDEFGHIJ
KLMNOPQRS
TUVWXYZ

abcdefghijklm
nopqrstuvwxyz

You weren't too happy about being at the beach. Especially when you got wet—the water was pretty cold. But who could resist naked baby pictures at the beach! We were at Capo Beach in California just under Great Grandma Ginn's house. The lighting was perfect and you were a trooper!

September 1999

PURE

Shaker

Sometimes your lettering just needs some space. Space to make a statement, stretch out and relax. Shaker does just that, and then some. It's casually sophisticated, elegantly whimsical and quietly bold.

Like the famous Shaker style, less is more, so be selective when choosing words to feature using this style. If you want the letters to roughly line up, pencil guidelines. Then sketch the basic shape of each character with a single line. Leave adequate space between letters. Now outline the letters so they are transformed into block-style characters.

The exaggerated widths of letters such as h, m and n are a key element of this style, so be sure to stretch them out. Note that most of the letter loops are wide open, especially in the letters a, b and g and that the middle line in the letters E and F are not connected to the rest of the character.

Creating Shaker can take no time at all, which means you can quickly move on to the fun part—filling in all those letters. Spread out your supplies because there's lots of room for variation. You'll find many uses for this style that works for most contemporary themes. Just give it some space!

Slant

Here's a fast lettering lesson. Start with a basic printed alphabet. Drop the lowercase f and s and every uppercase letter slightly below the baseline. Slant all horizontal lines and have them cross over the verticals. Leave the loops open. Now you have Slant, a tall, narrow style that allows you to fit a lot of words in a small space.

Of course there are more nuances to this lettering, but Slant teaches a valuable lesson: By changing a few details of an alphabet, you can come up with your own personalized lettering. All it takes is a little experimentation.

To re-create this lettering, start with guidelines to keep things generally straight. Pencil each character and finish with the pen color of your choice.

Notice that this style is meant to look like handwriting, so the lettering is not precise. Vertical lines in letters such as H and N are different heights. The crossovers extend beyond the vertical lines, like a quick scrawl. And the letters a, b, d and p are not perfectly joined, which adds to its casual feeling.

Aa Bb Cc Dd Ee Ff Gg

Hh Ii Jj Kk Ll Mm Nn

Oo Pp Qq Rr Ss Tt Uu Vv

Ww Xx Yy Zz

1 2 3 4 5 6 7 8 9 0

Christmastime

It's amazing how the cuzzies have grown when you add kids and husbands! Too bad Steve had to leave early.

The brothers and Steve relax after a wonderful Christmas dinner.

My Girls

I think I might be the luckiest mom around to be able to call two of the sweetest little girls I know my daughters.

The top reasons I know my girls love each other.

♥ Whenever Brinley cries, Alexa runs to get her baby doll and silky blanket for her.
♥ Whenever Alexa cries, Brinley pats her back.
♥ When Alexa sits on the couch to watch cartoons Brinley wants to sit right next to her.
♥ Brinley SQUEALS with delight whenever Alexa runs around.
♥ Alexa tells Brinley, "It's OK baby you be alright."
♥ When Brinley needs her diaper changed Alexa brings down a clean diaper without even being asked.

All For One

If you disliked grade-school grammar, here's your chance to break all the rules. Begin a sentence with a lowercase letter. Don't capitalize a proper noun. Even put uppercase letters in the middle of words. Shocking! And delightful.

If you can draw two parallel lines, you can write All For One lettering. Choose a letter height, draw two lines that distance apart, and pencil the characters between the lines. The greater the distance between your guidelines, the taller the letters appear.

Keep the letters as straight as possible. Emphasize the exaggerated elements such as the small half circle in the letter e and the tall ovals in the letters p, b and d. Variety is created by charming inconsistencies. For example, some curves, such as in the letters a and e and the number 6, are completed, while other curves in letters like g, j, s and t seem to stop short before they've completed the turn.

The best thing about All For One is its simplified approach. You only need one set of characters to convey the message, so why mess with upper- and lowercase? Just don't tell your English teacher.

abcdefghijkLm
nopqrstuvwxyz
1234567890

hemet high school
—class of seventy-six—

—25th—
reunion

i attended my 25th high school reunion on june 21, 2001 at the soboba country club all my friends were there. center then clockwise tony, sandy, cathy, laura, cathylee and me.

dillon played cornerback for the wildcats during the fall of 2000. they finished the season 5-4

COLUMBINE WILDCATS

LUCY LU BIGGLESWORTH
born october 12, 2000 • 1.5 to 18 pounds in just one year.

december 2000 3.5 pounds

february 2001 9 pounds

april 2001 12 pounds

december 2001 • 18 pounds

Contempo

Ever spin a yarn, tell a tall tale, or stretch the truth? As this lettering style illustrates, exaggeration can be an art. Stretching letter widths and vertical lines creates a classic, elegant look, and the lowercase letters provide a sophisticated understatement. With a few embellishments, however, this style easily adapts to a more whimsical theme.

This lettering can be easily mastered by practicing with a calligraphy pen. To keep the letters a consistent height, first lightly pencil guidelines. Holding the pen tip at a 45° angle, draw the lines of each letter using separate strokes.

For example, for the letter b, first draw the tall vertical line from the top to the bottom. Lift the pen from the paper and place the tip slightly up from the bottom. To complete the letter, draw the oval in a clockwise direction until it meets the bottom of the first stroke.

In general, draw the vertical lines from top to bottom, the curved lines from left to right and the round parts in a clockwise direction. Pay attention to exaggerating the widths of the letters h, m, n, s, u, v, w and x to capture the look of this alphabet. This style works particularly well when lettered along an arc or a curve. Simply use a journaling template to draw guidelines.

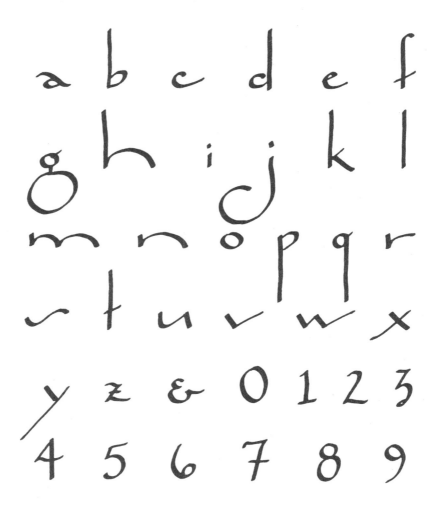

carole & harrison
dewegeli
dec. 20, 1958

to have and
to hold,
from this
day forward

a work of heart

Elegance

They say that opposites attract. Perhaps that's why the straight, asymmetrical fill-in areas of Elegance pair so well with its thin and curly lines. It's the contrast that appeals, like black and white, smooth and bumpy, sweet and salty.

If you think of Elegance as two distinct or opposite parts, it's much easier to create. In most cases you start with the fill-in area and then draw the curly lines. However, for round letters like C, G and O, and numbers such as 3, 6 and 9, draw the curved lines first and then the straight line for the fill-in space. The number 8 is simply one big double swirl.

Use penciled guidelines for both upper- and lowercase letters. For each columnar fill-in space, pencil-draw two straight and slanted lines, using a ruler as necessary. Close off the space with two horizontal lines that extend beyond the corners. Note that these asymmetrical areas taper up or down depending upon the letter. Complete each letter by drawing the thin curly lines.

Trace each penciled letter with a dark pen and color the fill-in areas as desired. Your page theme might suggest a coloring scheme or a variation for the swirls. Consider decorating with contrasting colors, patterns and textures.

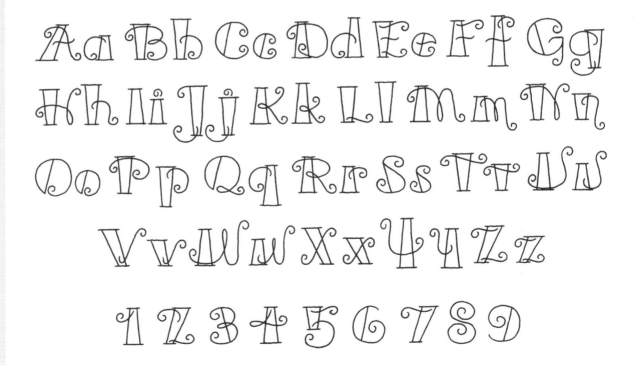

Whimsical Block

There's nothing symmetrical about this alphabet. The characters are different heights. The lines in each character are different lengths. In fact, this lettering is perfectly imperfect. But that's what gives it personality and gives you freedom to make mistakes. You can goof and nobody will notice. In fact, the more you tilt and slant, the better the look.

You can trace these block letters or easily draw them freehand. Using a pencil, draw each letter with single lines, varying the tops and bottoms so nothing appears to line up.

Leave adequate space between each character. Next, outline each letter, adding rectangular shapes at the ends of each line. When you are satisfied, trace each letter outline with a thin dark pen.

Perfect for contemporary photos or any page with a light-hearted theme, block letters like Whimsical Block beg for color, whether saturated hues from colored pens or the soft shades of colored pencils and watercolors. Experiment with different blending and shading techniques. If you make a mistake, no one will be the wiser, because it's supposed to be imperfect!

Juliann

If you've ever tied a locket of baby hair in a pretty ribbon and safely encapsulated it on a baby page, you'll instantly recognize the inspiration for this lettering. As wispy as those soft, strawberry blonde curls, Juliann letters almost look like they could be formed from individual strands.

Juliann has a casual, sketchy look that is designed to look imperfect. So your only challenge is to emulate the free-form style, not copy it exactly. Start with guidelines if you want the letters to loosely line up. Then sketch each letter, adding short crossbars and double lines where necessary. Notice that few of the lines meet; they either cross over or don't touch at all.

Trace the penciled letters with the pen color of choice and add color between the double lines if desired. You can get creative with the materials you use to create Juliann lettering but make sure the locks continue to look light and feathery as instant curls!

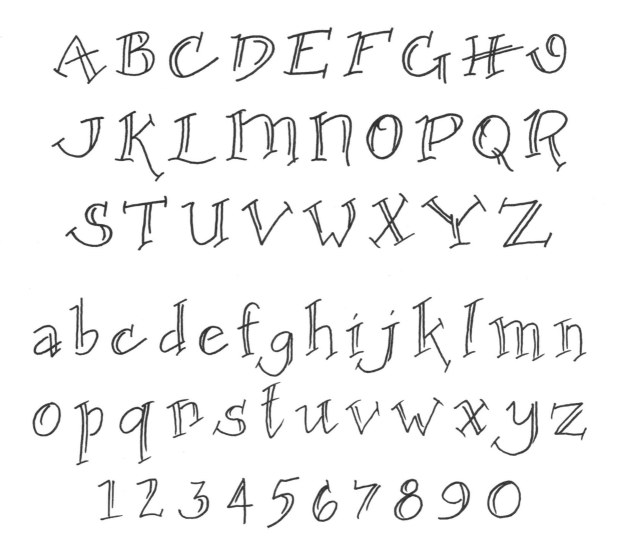

Laura's Graduation

Laura graduated from The Colony H.S. in May 2001. We were all there to watch her walk across the stage. She'll be attending Oklahoma State University in the fall. What a beautiful young woman she's become! Laura's heart belongs to the Lord; it's nice to know she won't be alone as she begins a new part of her life.

Special cousins... Laura and Julie

Alan on the drum

Laura crossing the stage

Marie, Mark
Mark, me, Laura, Julie, Grandmother Jackie Willie

Forever Friends

Twinkle Twinkle Little Star

Use Your Imagination

My New Ornament

Every year Julie gets an ornament from our former land-lady, Mrs. Carroll. Julie is very proud of ornament number four!

CHRISTMAS 1992.

Charity Ball

Dress is up. Dress it down. Fill it in. Leave it empty. Charity Ball is versatile enough to adapt to a variety of page themes.

The consistent heights and straight fill-in areas of this style make guidelines a necessity. Start by sketching each character with single lines. Note that the lowercase letters are extra tall, which gives the entire style a feeling of height. Also, some uppercase letters like A, B, D, R and S drop below the baseline, almost like dropped capitals.

To create the fill-in areas, simply draw one or two lines following the initial lettering guidelines.

You might prefer to use a ruler for this portion. Notice that each fill-in space is slightly tilted to the right. Look at the letter A, for example. If you connected the top left corner to the bottom right corner of the fill-in area, you'd end up with a straight line. This image may help you determine how steeply to slant each letter.

When you're happy with the sketched characters, trace them with a dark pen. Then color the fill-in areas, adorn them with texture and pattern, or simply leave them blank. Charity Ball works just about any way you design it.

FALL FUN

the many FACES of TIGGER

What's Cookin'?

The Aunties Shower

My mother threw me a beautiful dessert shower at our house on Friday night. I helped her make the dessert that day, and that beautiful flower was the perfect decoration. All the women "aunties" were there and the baby and I felt truly celebrated!

Since the weather had been so beautiful, we decided we'd try a bar-beque on the deck. It ended up being a bit of a disaster — the mari-nated veggies leaked everywhere and Tim tried to tame the grill with a fireplace poker.

I Believe...

Architecture

Those domestic goddesses who've had their share of laundry disasters know that the only way to salvage a favorite yet shrunken sweater is to dampen it and play tug-of-war with the now preemie-sized sleeves. Imagine doing the same with a basic uppercase alphabet and you've created Architecture lettering.

Every letter is expanded horizontally as if someone tugged and stretched each character as wide as it could go. For added flair, the S is stretched vertically. Because of its simplicity, this style works as well for captions as it does for titles. Its lack of embellishment also makes it a good choice for fast pages and masculine themes.

With the exception of the letter S, Architecture's uppercase letters fit between two parallel guidelines. Just determine the letter height and draw each character with exaggerated widths and angles. Note how the diagonal lines are stretched out in letters such as N and Y. The horizontal lines in the letters A, E and H are also lowered almost as far as possible.

To keep the letter widths consistent, try to match each width to the almost triangular letter A. Think about stretching that tiny sweater and you're on the right track.

Simple Stretch

Remember the popular childhood game Pick-Up Stix? You'd drop a wad of what looked like giant colored toothpicks on the floor, creating a random design. If that design actually formulated into letters of the alphabet, you'd see something that looked an awful lot like Simple Stretch.

The key to this alphabet is that each character is drawn with separate lines that cross each other at junctions. For example, the letter A is composed of three straight lines and three crossovers. The letter B includes one straight line, two curved lines and four crossovers. Notice that letters such as J and Y droop down noticeably below your baseline. The beauty of these characters is that the more crooked they are, the better they look.

If you focus on each line or curve rather than each letter, re-creating this style is a cinch. Just pencil in each letter and trace with black pen. Because it is not overly embellished, Simple Stretch works for both journaling and titles. Use this style alone for a simple, childlike effect, or dress it up with added decorations, like Easter eggs in the corner of each letter, to create something decidedly more festive.

ABCDEFGHIJKLM
NOPQRSTUVWXYZ
abcdefghijklmn
opqrstuvwxyz
1234567890

BALLET CLASS
The Love Of Dance

July 1998

Stephanie

heel   heel   toe

From the moment you could walk, you wanted to dance. You loved watching Barney and would dance along with whatever they were doing on the show. One evening while I was cooking dinner, you came in and asked me to dance with you. We danced all around the kitchen. After that day, I signed you up for dance class at the Barfield School of Dance. It amazed me that at 18 months you could follow so well. The teacher, Ms. Bonnie Neroth, even commented on how well you followed. These pictures were taken before we went to dance class. You are wearing your first dance outfit & tap shoes.

The Huntress

Ronnie Ron

1986-

Ronnie Ron was Roberta's little girl. She was named after the backup singer for Eddie Money, Ronnie Spector, which Robert liked. We nicknamed Ronnie "the Huntress" because she was always catching mice, squirrels, or any other small rodent that would come in the yard. The true protector of the yard. Ronnie Ron adored Robert and wherever he was, she was close by. At night, Ronnie would sleep on the pillow by Roberta's head. Robert cared for her and loved her very much.

ARTIST... EGGS-TRAORDINAIRE
Easter 2001

Final Art

Stephanie and Pam
Coloring Easter Eggs
Gigi Looking On

Stephanie's Easter Presents

Gigi

Stephanie and Mommy
Daddy looking on

You get so excited when holidays roll around and you especially love Easter. A couple of days before Easter, Gigi and Pam came over and colored eggs with us. This year you asked the Easter Bunny for your own scrapbooking supplies. You want to scrapbook like Mama and you are only four.

Curved Classic

Look closely. You won't find a single straight line. Although it seems too fancy to be easy, this lettering style is surprisingly simple because there's no perfect version of each letter. Nothing needs to be straight with this romantic, curvy style.

If you want the letters to generally line up, start with some guidelines. First lightly sketch or trace each letter with a pencil. Remember, all the lines are curved, so draw with a relaxed, loose hand.

Next, draw over the letter outlines with a thin dark pen. Color the fill-in parts of each letter with markers, pencils, watercolors, chalk or other supplies.

This style works well with a variety of themes from classic heritage to toddler antics. Keep the letters upright, or tilt them for fun and flair. Design the fill-in colors, patterns or textures to suit your page. Accent with decorative embellishments such as quilling, wire, and beads. However you create these curvy characters, you'll enjoy the freedom from sticking to the straight and narrow.

ABCDEFGHIJ
KLMNOPQR
STUVWXYZ

abcdefghij
klmnopqrs
tuvwxyz
1234567890

Grace

"Seemingly effortless beauty or charm of movement, form or proportion." There you have it—a definition of the word, "grace." It certainly applies to this lovely manuscript writing. The gentle curves and flowing lines of Grace lettering are equally appropriate for both titles and captions.

Mastering this style takes practice, but is well worth it. Begin by tracing the alphabet and numbers repeatedly on ruled notebook paper. Use the lines as a guide to keep the letters a consistent height. Notice how lowercase letters such as b, d and h are actually taller than the uppercase characters. The uppercase letters N, V, W and X have matching tall flourishes.

When you feel confident enough to create your own titles and captions, begin writing on penciled guidelines. Draw each character, revising as necessary. When finished, trace over the letters with a pen. The pen tip should be uniform because the lines in each character do not vary in width.

You'll find Grace an appealing style for any theme or time period. Its classic, handwritten look gives the impression that the words are worth the time it took to scribe them beautifully . . . gracefully.

Aa Bb Cc Dd Ee Ff Gg
Hh Ii Jj Kk Ll Mm
Nn Oo Pp Qq Rr Ss Tt
Uu Vv Ww Xx Yy Zz
1234567890

Puttin' on the Ritz

"High hats and narrow collars, white spats and lots of dollars." Irving Berlin's lyrics perfectly describe these tall, narrow letters with their elegant style and cool sophistication; however, they can dress down as easily as they can dress up.

Use a ruler and guidelines to keep the letters the same height and each character standing straight and tall. Start by penciling each character with a single line. Notice that horizontal lines are either "shoulder" high, as in the letters E, F and H, or "knee" low, as in the letters A and G. The lowercase t is also exaggerated in height.

Once you've sketched each letter, draw the outlines, taking care to keep the letter widths consistent. Use a ruler, as necessary, to keep the lines straight. Then trace and color each letter.

Puttin' on the Ritz is especially well-suited for cutting letters from solid or patterned paper. The lack of detail makes the cutting go faster, and the paper choice determines whether you end up with a simple, uncluttered caption or a fancy, sophisticated title. For extra glitz, outline each patterned letter with gold pen or sprinkle with glitter. À la Berlin, "you'll declare it's simply topping."

Hearts Entwined

Hearts for love, holly for Christmas, apples for school days, flowers for spring, snowflakes for winter. Whatever the theme, you can always create a matching design. Apply the idea to lettering and the result is this elegant, versatile style.

The hearts entwined concept is simple. Start with basic lettering and add themed doodles. These letters are fancy enough to use in separate letter boxes or as the featured first letter of a word or journaling paragraph.

When drawing or tracing these letters, start with guidelines to keep everything straight. Draw each character with single lines. Then go back and widen the thicker vertical parts. Once you're satisfied with the basic letters, draw over them with a dark pen, adding small triangles, or serifs, at the ends of each line.

For the doodled embellishments, pick up your pencil again. Combine swirls and dots with hearts, apples, holly leaves, snowflakes, flowers, or whatever fits your theme. Color over the thin lines with a dark pen and fill in the other shapes as desired.

Resources

The following companies manufacture products featured in this book. Please check your local retailers to find these materials. In addition, we have made every attempt to properly credit the trademarks and brand names of the items mentioned in this book. We apologize to any companies that have been listed incorrectly, and we would appreciate hearing from you.

3L Corp.
847-808-1140

Accu-Cut Systems®
800-288-1670

All Night Media®, Inc.
800-782-6733
(wholesale only)

American Tombow, Inc.
800-835-3232

Amscan, Inc.
914-345-2020

Artistic Stamp Exchange
800-232-5399

Broderbund
800-395-0277

Canson, Inc.
800-628-9283

Carolee's Creations
435-563-9336

Clearsnap, Inc.
800-448-4862

Close to My Heart™/D.O.T.S.
888-655-6552

Colorbök
800-366-4660

Colors by DESIGN
818-376-1226

The Crafter's Workshop
877-CRAFTER

Creative Beginnings
800-367-1739

Creative Memories®
800-468-9335

The C-Thru® Ruler Company
800-243-8419

Current®, Inc.
800-848-2848

Delta Technical Coatings, Inc.
800-423-4135

Design Originals
800-877-7820

DJ Inkers™
800-944-4680

Ellison® Craft & Design
800-253-2238

Extra Special Products Corp.
937-548-9388

The Family Archives™
888-662-6556

Family Treasures, Inc.
800-413-2645

Fiskars®, Inc.
800-950-0203

Folded Memories
425-673-7422

Frances Meyer, Inc.®
800-372-6237

Geographics, Inc.
800-426-5923

Hallmark Cards, Inc.
800-HALLMARK

Handmade Scraps
877-915-1695

Hero Arts Rubber Stamps, Inc.
800-822-HERO

Hot Off The Press®, Inc.
800-227-9595

K & Company
888-244-2083

Keeping Memories Alive™
800-419-4949

L Paper Designs
425-775-9636

Lake City Craft Quilling Supplies
417-725-8444

Making Memories
800-286-5263

Marvy Uchida
800-541-5877

resources

Mary Engelbreit® Studios
800-443-MARY

McGill, Inc.
800-982-9884

me & my BIG ideas
949-589-4607

Memory Makers® Memory Folding™,
Photo Kaleidoscopes™ and Punch
Your Art Out Volumes 1 & 2
800-366-6465

Microsoft® Corp.
microsoft.com

Michel® & Company
800-533-7263

MiniGraphics
800-442-7035

Mostly Animals Rubber Art Stamps
800-832-8886

MPR Associates®, Inc.
800-454-3331

Mrs. Grossman's Paper Co.™
800-457-4570

Northern Spy
530-620-7430

NRN Designs
800-421-6958
(wholesale only)

Paper Adventures®
800-727-0699

The Paper Company
800-426-8989

Paper House Productions
800-255-7316

Paper Parade
717-898-1212

The Paper Patch®
801-253-3018
(wholesale only)

Pebbles In My Pocket®
www.pebblesinmypocket.com

Pentel of America, Ltd.
800-421-1419

Personal Stamp Exchange
800-782-6738

Plaid Enterprises, Inc.
800-842-4197

Preservation Technologies
800-416-2665

PrintWorks
800-854-6558

Provo Craft
800-937-7686

Punkydoodles
800-428-8688

Puzzle Mates
888-595-2887

The Robin's Nest
435-790-5387

Royal Stationery™
800-328-3856

Rubber Monger
888-732-0086

Rubber Stamps of America
800-553-5031

Sakura of America
800-776-6257

Sandylion Sticker Designs
800-387-4215

SDL Corp.
509-476-4580

Sierra On-Line, Inc.®
800-757-7707

Sonburn, Inc.
800-527-7505

SonLight Press International
888-SON-LITE

SpotPen™ Hand Coloring Pens
505-523-8820

Stampabilities
800-888-0321

Stampendous!®
800-869-0474

Stampin' Up!
800-782-6787

Stamping Station, Inc.
801-444-3828

Stickopotamus®
888-270-4443

Suzy's Zoo®
800-777-4846

Uptown Rubber Stamps™
800-888-3212

Westrim® Crafts
800-727-2727

Index

index

the best in

wedding crafts & inspirations
from North Light Books, Memory Makers Books and Betterway Books!

Make your wedding a unique and memorable event!

You'll discover over 50 personalized projects to make your wedding one-of-a-kind. Easy-to-follow instructions guide you in creating professional-looking invitations and coordinated projects such as guest books, party favors, decorations, keepsakes and more. From whimsical and contemporary to elegant and sophisticated, you're sure to find inspiration to reflect your personal style for a wedding that is truly your own.

#70603-K • $19.99

Be sure to look for these wedding craft titles:

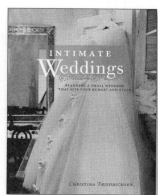

Intimate Weddings
#70642-K • $14.99

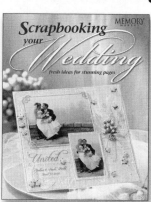

Scrapbooking Your Wedding
#33211-K • $22.99

New Inspirations in Wedding Florals
#70582-K • $19.99

How to Have a Big Wedding on a Small Budget
#70594-K • $14.99

The trusted source for brides-to-be

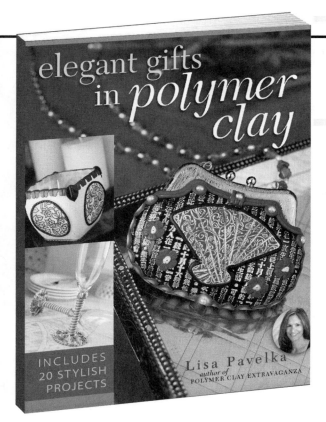

the best in
polymer clay techniques
from *North Light Books!*

Create Unique, Sophisticated Gifts!

Use the beauty and versatility of polymer clay to create elegant gifts your family and friends will adore. Lisa Pavelka guides you in creating 20 polymer clay projects using the latest techniques for a variety of stunning gift ideas in *Elegant Gifts in Polymer Clay.*

Through detailed direction you'll discover easy-to-follow methods for creating tortoise shell effects, rich enameled surfaces, the marbled look of mokumé gané, foil resists and faux mother-of-pearl. You'll use these techniques to create gifts such as a toasting goblet, a key rack, a votive candleholder and more!

#33028 • $22.99

Be sure to look for these polymer clay titles:

Clay Characters for Kids
#32161-K • $12.99

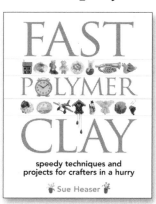

Fast Polymer Clay
#32703-K • $19.99

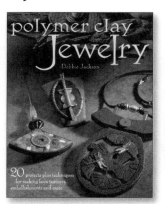

Polymer Clay Jewelry
#32873-K • $22.99

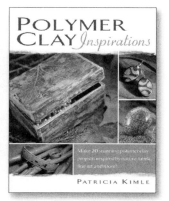

Polymer Clay Inspirations
#33013-K • $22.99

The trusted source for creative crafters

Savings Code
TL04EPCB

the best in
creative greeting cards
from *North Light Books!*

Create personalized greeting cards!

Renowned crafter MaryJo McGraw shares her most creative card ideas. With complete, step-by-step instructions and 23 detailed projects, you'll find it easy to make your sentiments more personal and meaningful.

#32580-K • $24.99

Be sure to look for these creative greeting card titles:

Vintage Greeting Cards with MaryJo McGraw
#32583-K • $23.99

Creative Correspondence
#32277-K • $19.99

Making Cards in a Weekend
#31665-K • $14.99

The Big Book of Handmade Cards and Gift Wrap
#33215-K • $21.99

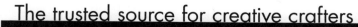

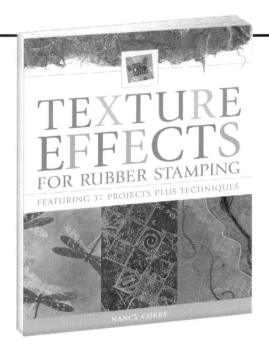

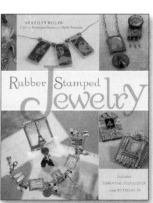